22,000+ BABY NAMES

BABY NAMES FOR GIRLS & BOYS

AMELIA KING

CONTENTS

PART II
BOYS NAMES

INTRODUCTION

THANK you for purchasing this baby names book, and congratulations! Whether you are a first-time parent or already have children, giving birth to new life is one of the most exciting times of a person's life.

We hope this extensive baby names list will help you find the perfect baby name for your special little one, and will be the last book you need on your journey to selecting a final name.

This book begins recently popular names. We have two lists of 40 of the most popular boys and girls names for 2019. Then there are two lists of the top 120 most popular baby girl and baby boy names for 2018. After that, you will find a list of more than 13,000 girls names, and more than 8,000 boys names.

In this ebook, you can navigate to specific letters through the table of contents, and find a link at the bottom of each page you view to take you back to the table of contents. This should make the book easy to browse. Don't forget to write down your favorites!

You can then look up your favorites later to find the meanings and popularity at bitly.com/namevoyager

We hope you enjoy, and one last note: If you enjoy this book, please take one minute to write a short review, as it helps us produce more quality books or see where to improve. You can leave a review by clicking HERE or visiting bitly.-com/namesreview. If you found an error in this book or have a suggestion for improvement, please email editor Katie Clark at contact@walnutpub.com.

Once again, thank you for buying, and congratulations on your exciting parenthood journey.

ON BABY NAMES MEANINGS

You may notice that we do not include baby name meanings and origins in this book. This is intentional. While meanings may, in popular baby names books, be made to seem all-important, I ask you to really think about how important a meaning ends up being to a name.

For example, how often has the meaning of your own name come up in your life? I'd guess not that often. Most people will never know the meaning behind your child's name, nor will they care. What is important about naming your baby is thinking about all the other factors that are more important, that will actually affect his or her life:

- How the name will position your child in their generation
- How the name will sound with their middle and last name
- How the name will go with your and your partner's name and any siblings
- What sort of pop culture or well-known associations the name has in people's minds

If you'd like to read more about how to choose a name for your baby, I recommend Aston Sanderson's "The Stress-Free Baby Names Book," which details just *how to choose* the name for your baby with a process that provides clarity, calm and confidence.

POPULAR GIRLS NAMES FOR 2019

Ada
  Amara
  Amelia
  Arabella
  Arya
  Aurora
  Ava
  Charlotte
  Ellie
  Emma
  Harley
  Harper
  Hazel
  Isabella
  Isla
  Kennedy
  Lucy
  Luna
  Maeve
  Malia
  Mila
  Natalie
  Nora
  Olivia
  Penelope
  Rylie
  Sadie

Sage Leia
Sasha
Savannah
Scarlett
Sofia
Stella
Thea
Violet
Zoe

POPULAR BOYS NAMES FOR 2019

Adam
   Alexander
   Asher
   Atticus
   Brandon
   Caleb
   Christopher
   Corin
   Daniel
   Declan
   Denim
   Dylan
   Elijah
   Emerson
   Everett
   Ezra
   Felix
   Finn
   Grayson
   Hunter
   Isaac
   Jack
   Jasper
   Jayden
   Joseph
   Kai
   Leo

Levi
Logan
Lucas
Mason
Nier
Oliver
Reuben
Rumi
Sebastian
Silas
Sir
Theodore
Xavier

TOP 120 GIRLS NAMES FOR 2018

Aaliyah
  Abigail
  Adalynn
  Adeline
  Alexa
  Alice
  Allison
  Alyssa
  Amelia
  Anna
  Aria
  Ariana
  Ariel
  Athena
  Aubree
  Audrey
  Aurora
  Autumn
  Ava
  Bella
  Brianna
  Brooklyn
  Camila
  Caroline
  Charlotte
  Chloe

Claire
Daisy
Delilah
Eleanor
Elena
Eliana
Eliza
Elizabeth
Ella
Ellie
Elsie
Emilia
Emily
Emma
Erin
Esme
Eva
Evelyn
Everly
Evie
Faith
Florence
Freya
Gabriella
Gianna
Grace
Grace
Hailey
Hannah
Harper
Hazel
Holly
Imogen
Isabella
Isabelle
Isla
Ivy
Jade
Jasmine
Jessica
Julia
Kayla
Kaylee
Kylie
Layla

Leah
Leilani
Liliana
Lillian
Lilly
Lily
Lola
Lucy
Luna
Madelyn
Madison
Matilda
Maya
Melanie
Mia
Mila
Millie
Molly
Naomi
Natalia
Natalie
Nevaeh
Nora
Olivia
Paisley
Penelope
Phoebe
Piper
Poppy
RaeLynn
Rosie
Ruby
Sadie
Samantha
Sarah
Savannah
Scarlett
Serenity
Sienna
Skylar
Sofia
Sophie
Stella
Valentina
Victoria

Violet
Willow
Ximena
Zoey

TOP 120 BOYS NAMES FOR 2018

AARON
Adam
Adrian
Aiden
Alexander
Alfie
Andrew
Angel
Anthony
Archie
Arthur
Asher
Austin
Ayden
Benjamin
Bentley
Braden
Brandon
Bryson
Caleb
Cameron
Carson
Carter
Charles
Charlie
Chase

Christian
Christopher
Colton
Connor
Daniel
David
Dominic
Dylan
Easton
Edward
Eli
Elias
Elijah
Ethan
Evan
Ezekiel
Ezra
Finley
Freddie
Gabriel
Gavin
George
Greyson
Harrison
Harry
Harvey
Henry
Hudson
Hunter
Ian
Isaac
Isaiah
Jace
Jack
Jackson
Jacob
Jake
James
Jason
Jaxon
Jaxson
Jayden
Jenson
Jeremiah
John

Jonathan
Jordan
Jose
Joseph
Joshua
Josiah
Julian
Kayden
Kevin
Kingston
Landon
Leo
Leonardo
Levi
Liam
Lincoln
Logan
Lucas
Luke
Mason
Mateo
Matthew
Max
Michael
Mohammed
Muhammad
Nathan
Nicholas
Noah
Nolan
Oliver
Oscar
Owen
Riley
Robert
Roman
Ryan
Samuel
Santiago
Sebastian
Teddy
Theodore
Thomas
Toby
Tyler

William
Wyatt
Xavier
Zachary

PART I

GIRLS NAMES

A

Aadi
Aafje
Aaid
Aaleila
Aalin
Aalis
Aaliya
Aaliyah
Aamna
Aanya
Aaralyn
Aarti
Aaryanna
Aasa
Aase
Aashna
Aasma
Aayah
Aayushi
Ababa
Abbey
Abbie
Abby
Abeba
Abeer
Abegale
Abelia

Abelie
Abella
Abelone
Abena
Aberdeen
Aberdine
Aberesh
Aberiana
Abernathy
Abha
Abhilasha
Abi
Abia
Abigael
Abigaia
Abigail
Abigaille
Abigale
Abihail
Abijah
Abilee
Abilena
Abilene
Abir
Abish
Abital
Abiya
Abra
Abria
Abriana
Abrianna
Abrie
Abriella
Abrielle
Abril
Abryanna
Absidee
Absylla
Abtar
Abygayle
Acacia
Acadia
Accalia
Acela
Acelina
Acelynn

Achara
Achsah
Acilia
Ada
Adabelle
Adaeh
Adafay
Adah
Adahlia
Adair
Adaira
Adaire
Adalaide
Adalee
Adalei
Adaleia
Adaleigh
Adalena
Adalene
Adalia
Adaliah
Adalie
Adalina
Adaline
Adaliss
Adaliz
Adaly
Adalyn
Adalynn
Adamaris
Adamina
Adania
Adara
Adaya
Adda
Addalie
Addica
Addie
Addien
Addy
Addyson
Adea
Adeara
Adecca
Adeeba
Adeen

Adél
Adela
Adelae
Adelaida
Adelaide
Adelaine
Adelajda
Adele
Adeleine
Adelfa
Adelheid
Adelia
Adélie
Adelin
Adelina
Adeline
Adelisa
Adelise
Adelissa
Adelita
Adeliza
Adell
Adella
Adelle
Adellene
Adelpha
Adelphia
Adelyn
Adelynn
Aden
Adena
Adepero
Aderine
Aderyn
Adhira
Adi
Adia
Adibella
Adica
Adie
Adiella
Adijah
Adilene
Adina
Adinda
Adira

Adisyn
Aditi
Adlee
Adleigh
Adlen
Adler
Adley
Adora
Adorabella
Adramicia
Adrastea
Adreen
Adria
Adrian
Adriana
Adriane
Adriani
Adrianna
Adrianne
Adrianny
Adrie
Adrielle
Adrienn
Adrienna
Adrienne
Adrijana
Adrina
Adrita
Adryen
Adsila
Adva
Adventura
Advirah
Adylin
Adyson
Aedith
Aegle
Aela
Aelfrida
Aelia
Aelin
Aelinn
Aelish
Aelita
Aelith
Aella

Aelwen
Aemilia
Aemy
Aenor
Aeria
Aerilyn
Aerin
Aerinn
Aeris
Aerith
Aeron
Aeryn
Aesinye
Aeva
Aeysha
Afifa
Afon
Afra
Africa
Afrodite
Afsaneh
Afsha
Afternoon
Afton
Agape
Agapi
Agata
Agatha
Agathah
Agathe
Agda
Aggie
Aglaé
Aglaia
Agnella
Agnes
Agnesina
Agnessa
Agneta
Agnetha
Agnija
Agnyetha
Agostina
Agota
Agueda
Agustina

Ahava
Ahinoam
Ahlai
Ahleya
Ahmeera
Ahmya
Ahnah
Ahnika
Aholibamah
Ahu
Ahuva
Ahyoka
Ai
Aia
Aibhne
Aibreann
Aïcha
Aida
Aidanne
Aide
Aidee
Aideen
Aiden
Aidenn
Aidyn
Aifric
Aignéis
Aikaterini
Aiko
Aila
Ailana
Ailani
Ailbhe
Aileen
Ailene
Ailey
Aili
Ailidh
Ailie
Ailís
Ailise
Ailish
Ailith
Ailla
Ailly
Ailsa

Ailynn
Aimee
Aimie
Aina
Ainara
Aine
Ainhoa
Aino
Ainslee
Ainsleigh
Ainsley
Ainslie
Airabella
Airam
Airene
Airianna
Airis
Airlie
Aisha
Aishla
Aishwarya
Aisla
Aislin
Aisling
Aislinn
Aislyn
Aislynn
Aitana
Aitzin
Aiva
Aixa
Aiyana
Aiyanna
Aiyla
Aizlynn
Aja
Ajani
Ajarae
Ajaya
Ajilea
Ajita
Ajooni
Akalroop
Akane
Akasya
Akayla

Akayna
Akela
Akende
Akenna
Akia
Akiah
Akiara
Akiko
Akilah
Akilina
Akina
Akira
Akiryana
Akiye
Akora
Alabama
Alachua
Alacia
Aladara
Alahna
Alaia
Alaina
Alaine
Alameda
Alana
Alanda
Alandra
Alane
Alani
Alanis
Alankrita
Alanna
Alannah
Alara
Alarice
Alaska
Alastríona
Alathena
Alauda
Alaura
Alaw
Alaya
Alayah
Alayna
Alaynah
Alayne

Alaysha
Alaysia
Alazra
Alba
Albania
Albany
Alberta
Alberte
Albertha
Albertina
Albertine
Albia
Albina
Albright
Alcee
Alchemy
Alcie
Alcyone
Alda
Aldabella
Alden
Aldis
Aldwina
Aleah
Aleanor
Aleasha
Alecia
Alecto
Aleda
Aleeah
Aleece
Aleelia
Aleen
Aleena
Aleesha
Aleesia
Aleeza
Alegria
Aleida
Aleigha
Aleise
Aleisha
Alejandra
Alejandrina
Alejhandra
Aleka

Aleksia
Alela
Alelia
Alena
Alene
Alenka
Aleny
Aleora
Alesana
Alesha
Aleshia
Alesia
Alessa
Alessia
Alesta
Alesya
Aleta
Aletha
Alethea
Aletheia
Alethia
Aletta
Alette
Aleu
Alev
Alex
Alexa
Alexana
Alexandrina
Alexea
Alexi
Alexia
Alexie
Alexina
Alexis
Alexius
Alexssa
Alexus
Alexxia
Alexys
Aleya
Aleyda
Aleydis
Alfa
Alfhild
Alfonsina

Alfreda
Alfrieda
Alheli
Ali
Alia
Aliah
Aliana
Aliandra
Alianna
Aliannah
Alianora
Alianore
Aliaya
Alibeth
Alice
Alicen
Alicenne
Alicia
Aliciana
Alicja
Alicyn
Alida
Aliena
Alienor
Alienore
Aliette
Alijah
Alika
Aliki
Alilia
Alina
Alinda
Aline
Alinnah
Alinya
Aliona
Alique
Alira
Alirah
Alisa
Alisabeth
Alisande
Alisann
Alise
Alisen
Alish

Alisha
Alisheba
Alison
Alissa
Alissandra
Alissia
Alisson
Alistar
Alisyn
Alita
Alithea
Alitheia
Alivia
Alix
Alixadria
Alixana
Alixandria
Aliya
Aliyah
Aliz
Aliza
Alizabeth
Alizandra
Alize
Alizée
Alizeh
Alizeia
Alizon
Alkelda
Alla
Allaire
Allana
Allayna
Allegra
Alleigh
Alleluia
Allene
Allese
Alleta
Allexis
Alleyah
Alleyne
Alli
Allie
Allira
Allirea

Alliree
Allison
Allissa
Allisson
Allisyn
Allora
Allorah
Allura
Allure
Alluryn
Ally
Allyn
Allysa
Allysen
Allyson
Allyssa
Allysyn
Alma
Almeda
Almeta
Almetrice
Almina
Almira
Almut
Alnaar
Alodia
Aloe
Aloha
Alohi
Aloisia
Aloma
Alona
Alondra
Alonna
Alora
Alouette
Aloysia
Alpana
Alpha
Alphonsine
Alphus
Alseta
Alsira
Alta
Altagracia
Altaira

Altalune
Altea
Altha
Althea
Altheda
Altheia
Alti
Alula
Alura
Alusengi
Alva
Alvard
Alvena
Alvera
Alverda
Alverta
Alvia
Alvina
Alvira
Alwilda
Alya
Alyana
Alyanna
Alyce
Alycia
Alyda
Alydia
Alyiah
Alyona
Alys
Alysa
Alysane
Alyse
Alyseca
Alysha
Alyshia
Alysia
Alyson
Alysondra
Alyssa
Alyssandra
Alyssha
Alyssia
Alyssianna
Alyssum
Alyvia

Alyviah
Alyx
Alyxandria
Alyxia
Alza
Alzbeta
Alzena
Ama
Amabel
Amable
Amada
Amadahy
Amadea
Amadora
Amae
Amaia
Amaiah
Amaira
Amaka
Amal
Amalea
Amalee
Amali
Amalia
Amalie
Amalina
Amalthea
Amalyah
Amana
Amanda
Amandeep
Amandeth
Amandina
Amandine
Amandla
Amani
Amantha
Amanthis
Amara
Amarachi
Amaranta
Amarante
Amaranth
Amarea
Amari
Amaris

Amarise
Amariss
Amarta
Amaryllis
Amaryllys
Amasa
Amata
Amatis
Amaya
Amba
Ambar
Amber
Amberlee
Amberleigh
Amberley
Amberlie
Amberlina
Amberly
Amberlyn
Amberlynn
Amberr
Amberson
Ambra
Ambre
Ambree
Ambria
Ambriel
Ambrielle
Ambrosia
Amedee
Amee
Ameera
Ameerah
Amefleur
Ameiah
Ameka
Amelea
Amelee
Ameleigha
Amelia
Ameliana
Amelie
Amelina
Ameline
Amelle
Amenpreet

Ameri
America
Americus
Amerie
Ameris
Amethyst
Ami
Amia
Amica
Amidala
Amie
Amiea
Amiee
Amiko
Amilia
Amina
Aminah
Aminatta
Aminda
Aminie
Amira
Amirah
Amisha
Amissa
Amita
Amitiel
Amity
Amiya
Amiyah
Amiyra
Ammara
Ammaria
Ammerie
Ammie
Ammorett
Amnah
Amora
Amorelle
Amoret
Amorette
Amoria
Amorie
Amory
Amparo
Amphitrite
Amrick

Amrit
Amrita
Amsala
Amsale
Amy
Amy Jo
Amy-leigh
Amya
Amyah
Amybeth
Amylia
Amylin
Amyrlin
Amzie
Ana
Ana-Lisa
Anaayah
Anabel
Anabela
Anabella
Anabelle
Anabeth
Anadelia
Anaëlle
Anah
Anaheed
Anahi
Anahid
Anahit
Anahita
Anaia
Anaiah
Anaïs
Anaiya
Anaiys
Anala
Analee
Analeigh
Anali
Analia
Analiese
Analilia
Analina
Analisa
Analise
Analisia

Analiz
Analuisa
Analyssa
Anamika
Ananda
Ananya
Anara
Anastacia
Anastella
Anastract
Anatalia
Anatola
Anatolia
Anaxandra
Anaxandria
Anaya
Anayah
Anberlin
Anca
Ancilla
Ancille
Andee
Andelyn
Andi
Andie
Andina
Andisheh
Andora
Andra
Andralissa
Andralyn
Andraste
Andrea
Andreanna
Andree
Andreea
Andreia
Andreina
Andreja
Andreva
Andri
Andria
Andriana
Andrianna
Andriette
Andrijana

Andrine
Andromeda
Andrzeja
Andy
Ane
Anea
Anechka
Aneesha
Aneira
Aneissa
Aneja
Anel
Anela
Anelie
Anelise
Anemone
Aneres
Anetta
Anette
Anezka
Anfisa
Ange
Angel
Angela
Angèle
Angelea
Angeleia
Angeles
Angelia
Angeliah
Angelica
Angelie
Angelika
Angeliki
Angelina
Angeline
Angelique
Angelise
Angelita
Angelle
Angelou
Angelus
Angelyn
Angelynn
Angenette
Angharad

Angie
Ani
Ania
Aniah
Anica
Anicka
Aniela
Anielia
Aniella
Anielle
Anieshka
Anika
Anikah
Aniline
Anina
Anisa
Anise
Anisha
Anissa
Aniston
Anistyn
Anita
Anitra
Anixsa
Aniya
Aniyah
Anja
Anjali
Anjanette
Anjela
Anjelica
Anjezë
Anju
Anjuli
Anka
Ankaret
Anke
Ankia
Anmei
Anmol
Ann
Ann Marie
Ann-Margaret
Anna
Anna-Blake
Anna-Maria

Annabel
Annabell
Annabella
Annabelle
Annabeth
Annacelli
Annagail
Annah
Annais
Annaleah
Annalee
Annaleigh
Annaley
Annalia
Annalie
Annaliese
Annalina
Annalind
Annalinda
Annalisa
Annalise
Annalyn
Annalynn
Annalysa
Annamae
Annamaria
Annamarie
Annanisa
Annapurna
Annasophia
Annastasia
Annastyn
Annbjørg
Anne
Anne Marie
Anne-Marie
Annebet
Anneka
Anneke
Anneli
Annelie
Annelies
Anneliese
Annelise
Annella
Annelle

Annelore
Annelyse
Annemarie
Annemie
Annemieke
Annerose
Annessa
Annessia
Anneth
Annetta
Annette
Anneya
Anni
Anni-frid
Annia
Annica
Annice
Annick
Annie
Annieka
Annierose
Anniina
Annika
Annikah
Annike
Anniken
Annikki
Annina
Annis
Annise
Annissa
Annisten
Anniston
Annmarie
Annona
Annora
Anny
Annystyn
Annytta
Anora
Anouk
Anousha
Anoushka
Anselee
Ansha
Anshi

Anslee
Ansleigh
Ansley
Anslie
Anthea
Anthee
Anthi
Anthoula
Antigone
Antinea
Antje
Antoinette
Antonela
Antonella
Antonetta
Antonette
Antonia
Antonie
Antonija
Antonina
Antonine
Anugraha
Anush
Anushka
Anvaya
Anwen
Anwyn
Anya
Anyssa
Anzhela
Anzhelika
Aobhe
Aoi
Aoibhe
Aoibheann
Aoibhinn
Aoibhne
Aoife
Aois
Aolani
Aomame
Aowyn
Aparna
Aphixia
Aphra
Aphrodite

Apolline
Apollonia
Apolonia
Apphia
Apple
April
April May
Aprille
Aprilynne
Apryl
Aqila
Aqua
Aquamarine
Aquaria
Aquila
Aquilina
Aquinnah
Ara
Arabel
Arabela
Arabella
Arabelle
Araceli
Aracelia
Aracely
Aradia
Araely
Araia
Aralia
Aralie
Aralyn
Arama
Aramie
Araminta
Aramya
Arana
Aranea
Aranka
Araseli
Arati
Aravis
Araxie
Araya
Arbor
Arbutus
Arcadia

Arcana
Arcanna
Arceli
Arcelia
Arcenia
Archana
Ardath
Ardell
Ardella
Ardelle
Arden
Ardent
Ardeth
Ardis
Ardita
Ardith
Ardolla
Areane
Areanna
Areanne
Areka
Areli
Arelis
Arella
Arelle
Arely
Aren
Arenda
Arete
Aretha
Arethusa
Areti
Areva
Arevik
Arezoo
Arezou
Argelia
Argentina
Aria
Ariadna
Ariadne
Ariagne
Ariah
Ariana
Arianda
Ariane

Arianell
Arianna
Arianne
Arianwen
Arianwyn
Aribelle
Arica
Arie
Arieana
Arieanna
Ariel
Ariela
Ariele
Ariella
Ariellah
Arielle
Arien
Arienne
Arieon
Arietta
Arilyn
Arin
Arina
Aris
Arisanna
Arisbe
Arisha
Arisia
Arissa
Arista
Aristea
Aristi
Arisu
Ariya
Ariyah
Ariyana
Ariza
Arizona
Arka
Arla
Arleen
Arlena
Arlene
Arlet
Arleth
Arlette

Arley
Arlie
Arline
Arlo
Arloa
Arly
Arlyn
Armanda
Armande
Armani
Armeetah
Armelle
Armeni
Armenouhi
Armi
Armida
Armina
Arminae
Arminal
Arminda
Armine
Arminta
Arnhild
Aroa
Aroha
Arpege
Arpi
Arpiar
Arpine
Arriane
Arrie
Arrietta
Arrietty
Arrinna
Arrow
Arsenia
Arsinoe
Artasia
Artemis
Arti
Artie
Aruna
Arvilla
Arwa
Arwen
Arya

Aryana
Aryanna
Arykah
Aryll
Aryn
Arynn
Arysta
Arzu
Åsa
Asalia
Asami
Asbjørg
Ascencion
Åse
Aselin
Asella
Asena
Asenith
Aseret
Asha
Ashalee
Ashanti
Ashari
Ashaya
Ashby
Ashe
Asheley
Ashely
Asheni
Asherah
Ashica
Åshild
Ashira
Ashlan
Ashland
Ashlea
Ashlee
Ashlei
Ashleigh
Ashlen
Ashley
Ashli
Ashlie
Ashlin
Ashling
Ashly

Ashlyn
Ashlynn
Ashten
Ashton
Ashtyn
Ashtynne
Asia
Asimina
Asiya
Asiyah
Asiye
Aska
Aslaug
Asli
Asma
Asmaa
Asmara
Asmira
Åsne
Aspasia
Aspen
Aspynn
Assala
Assisi
Assumpta
Assunda
Assunta
Asta
Astara
Astella
Aster
Asteria
Astero
Astghik
Astier
Astor
Astoria
Astra
Astraea
Astri
Astria
Astrid
Astrobella
Asuka
Asuna
Asuncion

Asya
Ataahua
Atabey
Atalanta
Atalante
Atalia
Atalie
Atalyn
Atara
Atarah
Ataya
Atha
Athalia
Athaliah
Athalie
Athanasia
Athena
Athenais
Athene
Atherton
Athia
Athlyn
Atia
Atira
Atita
Atiya
Atlanta
Atlantis
Atleigh
Atley
Atossa
Attica
Attie
Au'janae
Aubree
Aubreigh
Aubrey
Aubri
Aubriana
Aubrianna
Aubrie
Aubriel
Aubriella
Aubrielle
Aubrin
Aubry

Aubryn
Aubrynn
Aubuiny
Auburn
Aucella
Aud
Aude
Audecca
Auden
Audette
Audhild
Audie
Audny
Audra
Audre
Audrea
Audree
Audren
Audrey
Audria
Audriana
Audrianna
Audrie
Audrielle
Audrija
Audrina
Audris
Audru
Audry
Audryanna
August
Augusta
Auline
Aulora
Auneye
Aunika
Aunitra
Aunna
Aura
Aura-lee
Aurea
Aurelia
Aureliana
Aurelie
Aurembiaix
Auri

Auria
Auriah
Aurielle
Auristela
Aurnia
Aurora
Aurore
Aurorette
Aury Estela
Auryn
Auseta
Ausha
Ausinikka
Austėja
Austen
Austin
Austine
Australia
Austyn
Autiana
Automne
Autry
Autumn
Autumne
Auxane
Auxerre
Ava
Avabella
Avabelle
Avacyn
Avah
Avalanna
Avalee
Avaleigh
Avalene
Avaley
Avalie
Avalielle
Avaliese
Avalina
Avaline
Avalon
Avalyn
Avalynn
Avana
Avaneisha

Avanell
Avangeline
Avani
Avari
Avarie
Avaya
Avayah
Avdotya
Ave
Avelaine
Aveleigh
Avelina
Aveline
Avelyn
Aven
Aveni
Avenlee
Averi
Averie
Averiella
Averil
Averill
Averley
Avery
Aveson
Aveza
Avgi
Avgousta
Avha
Avia
Aviana
Aviance
Avianna
Avie
Avielle
Avigail
Avigayil
Avika
Avila
Avilynn
Avis
Avishai
Avital
Aviva
Aviya
Avlianna

Avoca
Avonlea
Avra
Avree
Avrey
Avrielle
Avril
Avrille
Avrora
Avua
Avy
Avyanna
Avyi
Avynn
Awilda
Awtry
Axelina
Axelle
Aya
Ayah
Ayaka
Ayala
Ayan
Ayana
Ayanda
Ayanna
Ayano
Ayasha
Aybree
Ayda
Aydan
Aydia
Aydon
Aydria
Ayeka
Ayelet
Ayesha
Ayisha
Ayla
Aylee
Ayleen
Ayleisa
Aylen
Aylin
Aymara
Aymeline

Ayn
Ayna
Ayolina
Ayriana
Ayşe
Aysha
Aysia
Ayslinn
Ayuna
Ayva
Ayzee
Azahara
Azalaïs
Azalea
Azalee
Azalei
Azalia
Azami
Azania
Azara
Azaria
Azelyn
Azenor
Azhar
Azie
Aziel
Aziliz
Azine
Aziyah
Aziza
Azni
Azuba

B

Baara
    Baby
    Baden
    Bagheera
    Baila
    Bailee
    Bailei
    Baileigh
    Bailey
    Bailie
    Báirbre
    Baisley
    Baize
    Baja
    Bakhshish
    Balbina
    Balbir
    Bali
    Baljinder
    Baljit
    Ballia
    Balqees
    Balvinder
    Balwinder
    Bama
    Bambi
    Ban

Banana
Bao
Barb
Barbara
Barbie
Barbora
Barbra
Barbro
Barcelona
Barra
Basanti
Basheera
Bashemath
Bashia
Basia
Basilia
Basilissa
Basimah
Basma
Bathilda
Batty
Batya
Baudelaire
Bay
Baya
Bayla
Baylee
Bayley
Baylin
Baylor
Bayrose
Bayusha
Bea
Beata
Beate
Beatrice
Beatrijs
Beatris
Beatritz
Beatriu
Beatrix
Beatriz
Beaue
Beaulah
Bebe
Bébhínn

Beca
Becca
Beckett
Beckie
Becky
Bedelia
Bee
Beeanka
Beezus
Begoña
Begonia
Behati
Beitris
Beka
Bekah
Belanna
Belem
Belen
Belia
Belicia
Belin
Belina
Belinda
Bell
Bella
Bella-Rose
Belladonna
Bellamy
Bellanne
Bellanore
Bellaria
Bellarosa
Bellary
Bellatrix
Belle
Bellefleur
Bellerose
Bellicent
Bellina
Bellis
Bellona
Belmira
Belora
Belphoebe
Belva
Beneve

Benevolence
Benicia
Benita
Benja
Benna
Bennett
Bennie
Bente
Bentley
Bentlie
Beracha
Berenice
Beret
Beretta
Bergljot
Berit
Berkeley
Berkleigh
Berkley
Berklie
Berlin
Bernadette
Bernadine
Bernardetta
Bernardine
Bernardita
Berneice
Bernice
Berniece
Bernita
Berta
Bertene
Bertha
Berthe
Bertie
Bertille
Bertina
Beryl
Bess
Bessa
Bessie
Bet
Beta
Beth
Betha
Bethan

Bethania
Bethany
Bethel
Bethena
Bethesda
Bethia
Bethiah
Bethsy
Bethzy
Beti
Betina
Betony
Betrys
Betsey
Betsy
Bette
Bettie
Bettina
Betty
Bettye
Bettylou
Beulah
Bev
Beverlee
Beverley
Beverlie
Beverly
Beverlyn
Bevin
Bexleigh
Bexley
Beyla
Beyoncé
Beyza
Bhavya
Bia
Bianca
Bianey
Bianka
Bianna
Bibi
Bibiana
Bibiane
Bice
Biddie
Biddy

Bijitha
Bijou
Bijoux
Bilaval
Bilhah
Biljana
Billie
Billie Jo
Billiejean
Billiejo
Billy
Billye
Bina
Bindi
Bindu
Biola
Bird
Birdee
Birdelle
Birdie
Birgit
Birgitta
Birgitte
Birleana
Birna
Birtha
Birtie
Biruta
Bissan
Bita
Bithiah
Bixenta
Bjork
Bjørg
Blair
Blaire
Blaise
Blake
Blakely
Blakelyn
Blakesly
Blanaid
Blanca
Blanch
Blanche
Blanchefleur

Blandina
Blandine
Blanka
Bláthnaid
Blayke
Blendenna
Blennie
Blerte
Blessing
Blessy
Blima
Bliss
Blithe
Blossom
Blue
Bluebell
Bluma
Bly
Blythe
Bobbette
Bobbi
Bobbie
Bobbie Sue
Bobby
Bobbye
Bodhi
Bodil
Bogdana
Boheme
Bojana
Bolina
Bolivia
Bonelle
Bonita
Bonnebell
Bonnie
Bonny
Bonnyjean
Boothe
Borbála
Borghild
Borgny
Boriana
Boston
Bostyn
Boudica

Bowie
Bracha
Bradi
Bradlee
Bradli
Bradlie
Brady
Braedyn
Braeleigh
Braelyn
Braelynn
Braeton
Brage
Braidy
Braila
Brailee
Brailey
Bráinne
Bralynn
Branca
Brandee
Brandi
Brandice
Brandie
Brandiwyne
Brandy
Brandywine
Branna
Brantlee
Branwen
Brave
Braxton
Braya
Braylee
Brayleigh
Braylene
Brayli
Brea
Breah
Breana
Breann
Breanna
Breanne
Breannon
Brecken
Breckyn

Breda
Bree
Breeanna
Breehanna
Breelyn
Breena
Breeshey
Breeze
Breezie
Breezy
Bregan
Brelan
Brelyn
Brenda
Brendalyn
Brendana
Brenley
Brenna
Brennan
Brenya
Brenyn
Breonah
Breonna
Breshay
Breslin
Brett
Bretta
Brettin
Brettlyn
Breydi
Bria
Briah
Briahna
Briahnna
Briallen
Brialli
Briana
Brianda
Briann
Brianna
Briannah
Brianne
Briannika
Briar
Briauna
Bricia

Brickley
Bríd
Brida
Bridget
Bridgett
Bridgette
Bridie
Brie
Briean
Brieana
Brieanna
Briege
Briela
Briella
Brielle
Briellen
Brienna
Brienne
Brierley
Brietta
Brigette
Brighid
Brighton
Brigid
Brígida
Brigit
Brigitta
Brigitte
Brilee
Briley
Brillana
Brille
Brilyn
Brilynn
Brin
Brina
Brinda
Brindle
Brinkley
Brinlee
Brinleigh
Brinley
Brinlie
Brinn
Brinxlee
Brinxley

Brionna
Briony
Briott
Brisa
Briseida
Briseïs
Brista
Bristol
Brit
Brita
Britain
Britannia
Britany
Britlyn
Britney
Britni
Britny
Britt
Britta
Brittan
Brittaney
Brittani
Brittanie
Brittany
Britten
Brittlan
Brittnee
Brittney
Brittni
Brittny
Britton
Brittyn
Brizzy
Brodie
Brody
Brogan
Bronagh
Bronte
Bronwen
Bronwyn
Bronya
Brook
Brooke
Browyn
Bruna
Brunilda

Bryana
Bryanna
Bryce
Bryelle
Brygid
Brylee
Bryleigh
Brylie
Bryliy
Bryluen
Bryn
Bryna
Bryndís
Brynhild
Brynja
Brynklie
Brynlea
Brynlee
Brynleigh
Brynli
Brynlie
Brynn
Brynna
Brynne
Brynnlee
Brynnley
Bryoni
Bryony
Brystal
Buena
Buffy
Bulah
Bunnie
Bunny
Bunty
Butterfly
Byrd

C

Cabernet
Cable
Cache
Cactus
Cadi
Cadie
Cady
Cadyn
Cadynn
Caecilia
Caedey
Caedran
Caedyn
Caela
Caeli
Caelia
Caelian
Caelyn
Caemlyn
Caetlin
Cai
Caia
Caidence
Caihong
Caila
Caileana
Cailee

Caileigh
Cailey
Cailie
Cailin
Cailla
Caily
Cailyn
Cailynn
Caina
Caisie
Cait
Caitee
Caitlan
Caitlann
Caitley
Caitlin
Caitly
Caitlyn
Caitlynd
Caitlynn
Caitria
Caitrian
Caitriona
Caiya
Calais
Calamint
Calandra
Calandre
Calantha
Calanthe
Calanthia
Calder
Caleah
Caledonia
Caleigh
Caley
Cali
Calia
Calianna
Calice
Calico
Calie
California
Calina
Calinda
Caliope

Calissa
Calista
Calixta
Calla
Calla Lily
Callalily
Calle
Calleigh
Calli
Callia
Callidora
Callie
Calliope
Callison
Callissa
Callista
Callisto
Cally
Callyn
Calogera
Calpurnia
Calybrid
Calypso
Calyse
Calyx
Camas
Camberlie
Cambree
Cambrey
Cambri
Cambria
Cambrie
Cambryn
Camden
Camdyn
Camea
Camelia
Camellia
Camelot
Cameo
Cameron
Cameryn
Cami
Camila
Camilla
Camille

Camillia
Camira
Camisha
Camlyn
Cammie
Cammy
Camora
Campbell
Camren
Camri
Camry
Camryn
Camylle
Cana
Canberra
Candace
Candela
Candelaria
Candess
Candi
Candia
Candice
Candida
Candis
Candra
Candy
Candyce
Canela
Canna
Cantarella
Cantrella
Canzada
Caoilainn
Caoilfhionn
Caoimhe
Capella
Capri
Caprica
Caprice
Capricia
Capucine
Capulet
Caquia
Cara
Carah
Caralea

Caraline
Caralyn
Caralynn
Cardella
Caren
Carenza
Caress
Caressa
Carey
Cari
Cariann
Cariba
Caridad
Carie
Carien
Carin
Carina
Carinda
Carine
Caris
Carisa
Carissa
Cariston
Carita
Caritas
Caritina
Carixia
Carla
Carlay
Carlee
Carleen
Carleigh
Carlene
Carley
Carli
Carlie
Carlin
Carlina
Carling
Carlota
Carlotta
Carlotte
Carlson
Carly
Carlyn
Carlyne

Carlynn
Carma
Carme
Carmel
Carmela
Carmelina
Carmeline
Carmelita
Carmelite
Carmella
Carmelliana
Carmen
Carmilla
Carmina
Carmindy
Carmyn
Carnie
Carol
Carola
Carolann
Carole
Carole-Anne
Carolee
Carolien
Carolina
Caroline
Carolyn
Carolyne
Carolynn
Caron
Carpathia
Carrabelle
Carrah
Carreen
Carri
Carrie
Carrigan
Carrington
Carrol
Carroll
Carryn
Carsci
Carson
Carsyn
Carsynn
Carter

Cary
Carya
Caryl
Caryn
Carynne
Carys
Casey
Cashlynn
Casi
Casia
Casidi
Casie
Casilda
Casimira
Caspara
Cass
Cassadee
Cassady
Cassara
Cassarah
Casse
Cassia
Cassidy
Cassie
Cassielle
Cassilda
Cassiopeia
Casslyn
Cassondra
Cassy
Castalia
Castielle
Cat
Catalaya
Catalena
Cataleya
Catalina
Catana
Catarina
Cate
Catelin
Cateline
Catelyn
Catelynn
Caten
Caterina

Catesby
Cath
Cathandra
Catharina
Catharine
Catherine
Catherynne
Cathey
Cathi
Cathie
Cathleen
Cathrine
Cathry
Cathryn
Cathy
Cati
Catie
Catina
Catlana
Catlin
Caton
Catreena
Catrin
Catrina
Catrine
Catrinel
Catriona
Cattleya
Caulfield
Cavielle
Cayanne
Caycee
Caydence
Cayenne
Cayla
Cayle
Caylee
Caylen
Cayley
Caylie
Caylin
Caynalin
Cayse
Caysie
Ce'Dana
Ceagan

Ceana
Ceara
Cebelle
Cecca
Cece
Cecelia
Cecil
Cecile
Cecilia
Cecilie
Cecillia
Cecily
Cecy
Cedar
Cedrella
Cedulie
Ceegan
Ceil
Céilidh
Ceinwen
Ceirra
Celaena
Celandine
Celene
Celenia
Celesta
Celeste
Celestia
Celestina
Celestine
Celia
Celiana
Celida
Célie
Celina
Celinda
Celine
Celisa
Celise
Celisse
Celyn
Celyse
Cenda
Cenia
Centaine
Century

Ceola
Cerci
Ceredwyn
Ceres
Ceri
Ceridwen
Cerie
Cerina
Ceris
Cerise
Cerissa
Cersei
Cerys
Cesalie
Cesara
Cesaria
Cesarina
Cesca
Ceslee
Cesli
Cessair
Cessily
Cessy
Ceychelle
Ceylan
Cezanne
Chaiza
Chalice
Challen
Chamari
Chambray
Chamya
Chana
Chanae
Chanda
Chandell
Chandler
Chandley
Chandra
Chandry
Chanel
Chanelle
Chani
Chanin
Channah
Channary

Channing
Channon
Chantal
Chante'
Chantel
Chantella
Chantelle
Chantia
Chantilly
Chantol
Chapel
Chapen
Chaperel
Chappell
Chara
Charaya
Chardé
Chardonnay
Chari
Charidan
Charilette
Charis
Charisa
Charisma
Charissa
Charisse
Charitina
Charitini
Charity
Charla
Charlaine
Charlayne
Charlea
Charlee
Charleen
Charleigh
Charlene
Charleston
Charley
Charli
Charlianne
Charlie
Charliene
Charline
Charlize
Charlotta

Charlotte
Charlsie
Charly
Charmae
Charmaine
Charmian
Charminique
Charmion
Charnette
Charnjot
Charolette
Charsey
Charvala
Charys
Chasadee
Chase
Chaselynn
Chasey
Chasity
Chassidy
Chastity
Chasya
Chauncey
Chava
Chavela
Chavelly
Chaya
Chayka
Chaylee
Chayna
Chaynee
Chayo
Chedva
Chela
Chelan
Chelcie
Chelidon
Chella
Chelle
Chellsie
Chelly
Chelo
Chelsea
Chelsee
Chelsey
Chelsi

Chelsia
Chelsie
Chencha
Chenelle
Cheney
Chenne
Chenoa
Chepa
Cher
Chera
Chere
Cherelle
Cheri
Cherie
Cherilyn
Cherine
Cherise
Cherish
Cherith
Cherline
Cherlynn
Cherrelle
Cherri
Cherrie
Cherry
Cheryl
Cheryle
Cheryll
Chesapeake
Cheshmeh
Cheska
Cheslai
Chesney
Chesten
Chestina
Chevaune
Chevelle
Chevonne
Cheyanna
Cheyanne
Cheyenne
Cheyne
Chiaki
Chiana
Chianne
Chiara

Chiarina
Chica
Chie
Chihiro
Chiles
Chimène
China
Chinesa
Chionia
Chiori
Chiquinquira
Chiquita
Chivon
Chloann
Chloe
Chloey
Chloris
Cho
Chole
Choncha
Chrethe
Chrimzen
Chris
ChrisAnna
Chrisette
Chrisial
Chrissa
Chrissey
Chrissie
Chrissy
Christa
Christabel
Christabella
Christabelle
Christal
Christany
Christeanna
Christeen
Christel
Christella
Christelle
Christen
Christena
Christene
Christi
Christia

Christian
Christiana
Christiane
Christiania
Christianna
Christianne
Christie
Christin
Christina
Christine
Christophe
Christy
Christyl
Christyn
Chritiane
Chryne
Chrysa
Chrysalis
Chrysania
Chula
Chunda
Chuya
Chyane
Chyanne
Chyenne
Chyler
Chyna
Chynna
Ciana
Ciandra
Cianna
Ciar
Ciara
Ciaran
Ciarran
Cicada
Cicca
Cicely
Cidelle
Cidnee
Ciela
Cielle
Cielo
Ciena
Ciendauos
Cienna

Ciera
Cierra
Cierrin
Cilinia
Cilla
Cimorene
Cinda
Cindal
Cindel
Cinderella
Cindi
Cindra
Cindric
Cindy
Cinnamon
Cinthia
Cinthya
Cintia
Cinxia
Cinzia
Ciorstaidh
Circe
Cirie
Cissy
Citana
Citlali
Citlalli
Citrine
Citron
Clacie
Cladine
Clair
Clair-de-lune
Claira
Claire
Claireece
Clairese
Clairey
Clancey
Clancy
Clara
Clarabella
Clarabelle
Clarah
Clare
Claren

Clarencia
Claret
Claria
Claribel
Clarice
Clarie
Clariel
Clarimond
Clarina
Clarinda
Clarine
Clarinell
Claris
Clarisa
Clarissa
Clarisse
Clarita
Clarity
Clarizza
Clark
Clarke
Clary
Clasina
Claude
Claudean
Claudette
Claudia
Claudie
Claudina
Claudine
Clavel
Clea
Clelia
Clélie
Clely
Clematis
Clémence
Clemencia
Clemency
Clementina
Clementine
Clemmie
Cleo
Cleone
Cleopatra
Cleora

Cleotha
Cleotilde
Cleta
Clidhna
Clio
Cliodhna
Cliona
Clochette
Clodagh
Cloe
Clora
Clorinda
Cloris
Clothilde
Clotilda
Clotilde
Clotille
Clove
Clover
Clyda
Clymene
Clytie
Cobie
Cocheta
Cochrann
Coco
Cocoa
Codi
Codie
Cody
Coelee
Coeli
Colbie
Colby
Coleen
Coletta
Colette
Coley
Colie
Coline
Colleen
Collette
Collins
Collyn
Columba
Columbia

Columbine
Comfort
Conceicao
Concepcion
Concetta
Concha
Conchita
Concordia
Conner
Connery
Conni
Connie
Connolly
Constança
Constance
Constancia
Constantia
Constantina
Constanza
Constanze
Consuela
Consuelo
Contessa
Copeland
Coppelia
Copper
Cora
Corabel
Corabella
Corabelle
Coraima
Coral
Coralee
Coralia
Coralie
Coralina
Coraline
Coralise
Coralye
Coralynne
Coranne
Corazon
Corda
Cordelia
Cordella
Cordessa

Cordia
Cordie
Corealana
Coree
Coreen
Coreene
Corelia
Corella
Corene
Coretta
Corette
Corey
Cori
Coriander
Corie
Corina
Corine
Corinna
Corinne
Corinth
Corinthia
Corisande
Corissa
Corissia
Corita
Corky
Corla
Corliss
Cornelia
Corona
Corran
Correene
Corri
Corriana
Corrie
Corrigan
Corrine
Corryn
Cortana
Cortney
Cortnie
Corva
Cory
Coryn
Corynn
Cosette

Cosima
Cosma
Cosmina
Costanza
Courey
Courtenay
Courteney
Courtland
Courtlin
Courtlyn
Courtlynn
Courtney
Cova
Coya
Cozette
Creda
Cree
Creeda
Creola
Cresanna
Crescence
Crescencia
Crescent
Crescentia
Cresence
Cressa
Cressida
Cricket
Crimson
Crisiant
Crispina
Crissy
Crista
Cristabel
Cristabell
Cristal
Cristalyn
Cristela
Cristen
Cristiana
Cristin
Cristina
Cristy
Cruella
Crunchi
Cruz

Crysta
Crystal
Crystal-Rose
Csilla
Cuca
Currin
Curry
Cwen
Cyan
Cyane
Cybele
Cybil
Cydnee
Cydney
Cydonia
Cyleigh
Cymani
Cymbre
Cynara
Cyndee
Cyndi
Cyndy
Cynlee
Cynorah
Cyntha
Cynthia
Cynthianna
Cypress
Cyra
Cyrille
Céline

D

Da-xia
Dabney
Dacey
Daci
Dacia
Daciana
Dacy
Daegan
Daeja
Daela
Daelyn
Daenerys
Dafna
Dafne
Dafni
Daggi
Dagmar
Dagmara
Dagny
Dahl
Dahlia
Dahyun
Daiana
Daija
Dailey
Daily

Dailyn
Daire
Dairrica
Daisey
Daisha
Daisia
Daisy
Daisy-Mae
Daiya
Daja
Dakota
Dalary
Dale
Dalee
Dalena
Daleyza
Dalia
Dalila
Dalilah
Dalinda
Dalisay
Dalisha
Daliyah
Dallace
Dallas
Dallis
Dallyce
Dalma
Dalya
Damara
Damaris
Damhnait
Damiana
Damiane
Damita
Dana
Danae
Danaiah
Danalyn
Danara
Danataya
Danaya
Danby
Daneen
Daneira

Danelle
Danesah
Danette
Daneysha
Danger
Dani
Dania
Danica
Daniela
Daniele
Daniella
Danielle
Danijah
Danijela
Danika
Danila
Danita
Daniyah
Danjela
Danna
Danneel
Dannie
Danniella
Dannielle
Dannika
Dannyn
Danteja
Danu
Danuta
Danya
Danyelle
Daphene
Daphna
Daphne
Daphnée
Daphnie
Dara
Daralyn
Darbi
Darbiana
Darbie
Darby
Darcella
Darcey
Darcey-Mae

Darci
Darcie
Darcy
Daria
Darian
Dariela
Darien
Darja
Darky
Darla
Darleen
Darlena
Darlene
Darletta
Darley
Darlin
Darline
Darlynn
Darquise
Darra
Darrah
Darreth
Darryn
Darshan
Darthula
Darya
Daryl
Daryon
Dasha
Dashielle
Dasia
Dassah
Datha
Daton
Dava
Davalyn
Davanee
Daveigh
Daveney
Davette
Davia
Daviana
Davida
Davina
Davinder

Davinee
Davita
Dawn
Dawna
Dawnalee
Dawsyn
Day
Daya
Dayami
Dayan
Dayana
Dayanara
Dayja
Dayla
Dayle
Daylee
Dayleigh
Daylen
Dayna
Dayne
Dayton
Daytona
Dayvee
Dea
Dean
Deana
Deandra
Deangela
Deanica
Deann
Deanna
Deanndra
Deanne
Dearbhail
Dearbhla
Deasia
Deb
Debbi
Debbie
Debbra
Debby
Debelah
Debi
Debjani
Debora
Deborah

Debra
Debrah
December
Dedra
Dee
DeeAnn
DeeAnna
Deedee
Deena
Deepti
Defne
Deianira
Deidamia
Deidra
Deidre
Deirdre
Deisy
Deja
Dejah
Dejalena
Dejanae
Dejani
Dejanira
Dejianna
Dekotha
Delaina
Delaine
Delainey
Delana
Delancey
Delancy
Delaney
Delanie
Delany
Delara
Delayne
Delen
Delenn
Delentha
Deletha
Delfina
Delfine
Delgadina
Delia
Deliah
Delicia

Delight
Delila
Delilah
Delina
Delisa
Delisha
Dell
Della
Delma
Delois
Delora
Delores
Deloris
Delpha
Delphia
Delphina
Delphine
Delphinia
Delphinium
Delta
Delun
Delwyn
Delylah
Delyn
Delysia
Delyth
Dema
Demaris
Demelza
Demeter
Demetra
Demetria
Demetrice
Demi
Demitra
Dena
Denali
Denaye
Denbeigh
Denee
Deneen
Deni
Denia
Denice
Denielle
Denika

Denine
Denisa
Denise
Denisha
Denisia
Denisse
Deniz
Denna
Dennise
Dennon
Denya
Deogracia
Deolinda
Deondra
Deonna
Dereka
Dervla
Deryn
Desdemona
Deshae
Desi
Desideria
Desirae
Desiray
Desire
Desirea
Desiree
Desirie
Desislava
Desneiges
Despina
Dessa
Dessie
Dessy
Desta
Destanee
Destany
Destinee
Destiney
Destini
Destinie
Destiny
Destri
Destyni
Deva
Devan

Devanie
Devannie
Devany
Devanya
Deven
Devere
Devereaux
Devi
Devin
Devina
Devinder
Devinne
Devlyn
Devoireh
Devon
Devona
Devonie
Devonne
Devony
Devora
Devorah
Devorgilla
Devra
Devri
Devyn
Dewayna
Dexlee
Deyanira
Deyna
Dezabia
Dezirae
Deziraye
Dezzie
Dganit
Dhana
Dharani
Dharma
Dhriti
Di
Dia
Diadama
Diamanda
Diamanta
Diamanto
Diamira
Diamond

Dian
Diana
Diancia
Diandra
Diane
Dianella
Dianey
Diann
Dianna
Dianne
Dianora
Diantha
Diara
Diavian
Dicey
Dicy
Didina
Dido
Diedre
Diem
Digna
Dileyna
Dillen
Dillon
Dillyn
Dilys
Dimitra
Dimitri
Dimitroula
Dimity
Dimple
Dina
Dinah
Dinalee
Dinara
Dinella
Dineo
Dinesha
Dinh
Dinitia
Dinorah
Dione
Dionna
Dionne
Diora
Diotima

Disa
Dita
Divanshi
Diviana
Divina
Divine
Divinity
Divya
Dixie
Diya
Djuna
Dmitriana
Docia
Dodai
Dodie
Doireann
Doliana
Dolla
Dolley
Dollie
Dolly
Dolorea
Dolores
Doloris
Dolorosa
Dolphin
Domenica
Domicela
Dominga
Domini
Dominica
Dominika
Dominique
Domino
Dominque
Domonique
Dona
Donata
Donatella
Donea
Donel
Donella
Donelle
Donia
Doniella
Donielle

Donita
Donna
Donna Jo
Donnelly
Donnie
Doone
Dora
Doraine
Dorathy
Dorcas
Dorea
Doreen
Doreena
Dorene
Dorete
Doretha
Dori
Doria
Dorian
Doriana
Doriane
Dorianne
Dorina
Dorinda
Dorine
Doris
Dorit
Dorka
Dorla
Dorota
Dorotea
Dorotha
Dorothea
Dorothy
Dorotta
Dorottya
Dorrie
Dorrin
Dorris
Dorry
Dorte
Dortha
Dorthy
Dory
Doshia
Doshie

Dot
Dottie
Dotty
Doutzen
Dove
Dovey
Dovie
Draden
Dragana
Drametha
Drea
Dream
Dreama
Dree
Drema
Dresden
Drew
Drienne
Drishya
Drita
Dru
Drucilla
Drue
Druscilla
Drusilla
Dua
Duana
Dufa
Dulce
Dulcia
Dulciana
Dulcibella
Dulcie
Dulcina
Dulcinea
Dunia
Dunja
Dusta
Dusti
Dustina
Dusty
Dutchess
Dvorah
Dwynwen
Dyan
Dyani

Dyann
Dyanna
Dylan
Dylana
Déja

E

Eadoin
Eara
Earnestine
Eartha
Eastan
Easter
Eastleigh
Easton
Eavan
Eaven
Ebba
Ebbie
Ebonee
Eboni
Ebonnie
Ebony
Ebrill
Ebru
Ecaterina
Echo
Eda
Edana
Edda
Eddie
Edel
Edele

Edelia
Edeline
Edelle
Edelmira
Edelweiss
Eden
Edie
Edina
Edita
Edith
Editta
Edmonia
Edna
Edoliah
Edrie
Eduarda
Eduwiges
Edviga
Edvige
Edward
Edwardine
Edwige
Edwina
Edye
Edyta
Edyth
Edytha
Edythe
Eevee
Eevi
Efa
Effie
Effy
Efrat
Efthimia
Eftychia
Eglantine
Egypt
Eibhlín
Eidel
Eija
Eila
Eilah
Eilan
Eilat
Éile

Eileen
Eileene
Eiley
Eiliana
Eilidh
Eilika
Eilinora
Éilís
Eilish
Eiliyah
Eilonwy
Eiluned
Eilwen
Eily
Eimear
Eira
Eireann
Eirene
Eirian
Eirin
Eirini
Eirlys
Eirwen
Eiry
Eisla
Eisley
Eislyn
Eithne
Eivet
Ekaterina
Ekaterini
Ela
Elaina
Elaine
Elais
Elana
Elani
Elanna
Elanor
Elanora
Elaphia
Elara
Elaria
Elaura
Elayna
Elayne

Elba
Elberta
Elda
Eldbjørg
Eldora
Eléa
Eleana
Eleanna
Eleanor
Eleanora
Eleanore
Elearie
Elease
Electa
Electra
Eleena
Eleftheria
Eleisha
Elektra
Elen
Elena
Elene
Eleni
Elenia
Elenka
Elenna
Elenor
Elenora
Elenore
Eleonoora
Eleonora
Eleonore
Eleora
Eleri
Elery
Elessa
Elestren
Eletha
Elettra
Elexandra
Elexena
Elexia
Elexina
Elexine
Elfa
Elfie

Elfleda
Elfreda
Elfrida
Elfrieda
Elfriede
Eli
Elia
Eliamar
Eliana
Eliane
Elianna
Eliarys
Elida
Elidia
Eliette
Elif
Eliisa
Elin
Elina
Elinda
Eline
Elinor
Elinora
Elinore
Eliora
Eliot
Eliotte
Elira
Elisa
Elisabelle
Elisabet
Elisabeta
Elisabeth
Elisabetha
Elisabetta
Elisabette
Elisangela
Elisavet
Elise
Elisha
Elisheba
Elisheva
Elisia
Eliska
Elissa
Elissia

Elithea
Elitsa
Elivia
Elixane
Eliya
Eliza
Elizabell
Elizabella
Elizabelle
Elizabeta
Elizabeth
Elizandra
Elizaveta
Elize
Elizebeth
Elka
Elke
Ella
Ella-mae
Elladora
Ellajean
Ellamae
Ellar
Ellasyn
Elle
Ellea
Elleanor
Ellen
Ellena
Ellenie
Ellenor
Elleny
Ellerie
Ellery
Ellesa
Ellessa
Ellexa
Ellexis
Elli
Ellia
Elliana
Ellianna
Ellias
Elliauna
Ellicia
Ellie

Ellieana
Ellieka
Elliette
Ellika
Ellin
Ellina
Ellinette
Ellington
Ellinor
Elliot
Elliott
Elliotte
Ellis
Ellisia
Ellison
Elliw
Elliya
Elloa
Elloise
Ellone
Ellora
Ellorie
Ellory
Ellowyn
Elly
Ellyn
Ellysia
Elma
Elmera
Elmira
Elna
Elnara
Elnora
Elodia
Elodie
Eloina
Elois
Eloisa
Eloise
Elona
Elora
Elorah
Eloriah
Elouera
Elouise
Elowen

Elowyn
Elphaba
Elpida
Elsa
Elsabeth
Elsanna
Elsbeth
Else
Elsha
Elsie
Elsje
Elspet
Elspeth
Elsy
Elta
Elula
Eluned
Elva
Elvah
Elvera
Elvia
Elvie
Elvina
Elvira
Elvire
Elvisa
Elwy
Elwyn
Elya
Elyanna
Elyannah
Elyia
Elynn
Elynor
Elyon
Elyse
Elysha
Elysia
Elysian
Elyssa
Elysse
Elyvia
Elza
Elzbieta
Elzi
Elzina

Ema
Emaan
Emagine
Emalee
Emalei
Emalina
Emaline
Emallie
Emalyn
Eman
Emanuela
Emanuella
Emanuelle
Emarie
Ember
Emberlain
Emberlee
Emberley
Emberly
Emberlyn
Emberlynn
Embeth
Embla
Emblyn
Embrace
Embry
Emele
Emeleth
Emeli
Emelia
Emeliana
Emelie
Emelina
Emeline
Emelissa
Emelisse
Emely
Emelyn
Emer
Emerald
Emeraude
Emeria
Emerie
Emerson
Emersyn
Emery

Emeryn
Emese
Emi
Emica
Emika
Emiko
Emila
Emilee
Emileigh
Emilia
Emiliana
Emilie
Emilija
Emilina
Emilly
Emily
Emilyn
Emilynne
Emina
Emira
Emiri
Emlyn
Emma
Emmalie
Emmalina
Emmaline
Emmalise
Emmaly
Emmalyn
Emmalynn
Emmanuelle
Emmarie
Emmary
Emme
Emmit
Emmlyn
Emmy
Emmylou
Emogen
Emogene
Emőke
Emorie
Emory
Empress
Emree
Emrick

Emry
Emsley
Emy
Emyli
Ena
Encarnacion
Endellion
Endelyn
Endora
Enedelia
Enedina
Eneida
Eneroliz
Enfys
Engelisa
Engla
English
Engracia
Enid
Eniola
Enity
Enjoli
Enna
Enni
Enola
Enora
Enrica
Enriqueta
Enya
Enyo
Eoduin
Eos
Eowyn
Ephie
Ephrath
Ephtehia
Epiphany
Epona
Eponine
Eppie
Era
Erato
Ercilia
Erela
Erendira
Ereni

Eriah
Eriana
Erianna
Erica
Ericha
Ericka
Erie
Eriel
Eriella
Erielle
Erika
Eriko
Erilyn
Erin
Erinn
Erinna
Eris
Erisa
Erissa
Erista
Erith
Eriu
Erlene
Erlinda
Erline
Erma
Ermelinda
Ermengarde
Erminia
Ermintrude
Ermioni
Erna
Ernestina
Ernestine
Erowyn
Errika
Errin
Errol
Ersilia
Eryn
Erynn
Erynne
Erzsébet
Esabella
Eseld
Esfir

Esha
Esiree
Eskai
Eslanda
Esma
Esmae
Esme
Esmee
Esmeralda
Esmeray
Esmerie
Esmira
España
Esperance
Esperanza
Esphyr
Esra
Esra'a
Essalie
Essence
Essie
Essra
Esta
Estée
Estefana
Estefani
Estefania
Estefany
Estela
Estelia
Estell
Estella
Estelle
Estember
Ester
Estera
Esteri
Esterina
Esther
Esti
Estibaliz
Estivalis
Estrella
Estrellita
Estrild
Esty

Esyllte
Eszter
Eszti
Etahjayne
Étaín
Etelka
Eternity
Etha
Ethel
Ethelene
Ethelyn
Ethelyne
Ethna
Ethne
Ethney
Ethnie
Ethyl
Ethylene
Etna
Etoile
Etta
Ette
Ettie
Ettien
Euanthe
Eudocia
Eudora
Eudosia
Eudotia
Eudoxia
Eudoxie
Eufemia
Eufrasia
Eufrozina
Eugenia
Eugenie
Eula
Eulah
Eulala
Eulalia
Eulalie
Euletta
Euna
Eunice
Eunicia
Euniecia

Euodia
Eura
Europa
Eurydice
Eusebia
Eustacia
Eva
Eva Marie
Eva-Lynn
Evabelle
Evadne
Evalee
Evaleigh
Evalie
Evalina
Evaline
Evalinn
Evalyn
Evalynn
Evalynne
Evan
Evaña
Evandra
Evanee
Evanesca
Evangalista
Evangelia
Evangelica
Evangelina
Evangeline
Evangelique
Evangelynn
Evania
Evann
Evanna
Evanne
Evanora
Evanthe
Evanthia
Evany
Evarista
Evdokia
Evdokiya
Evdoxia
Eve
Eve-Marie

Evedene
Eveleen
Evelia
Evelien
Evelin
Evelina
Eveline
Eveling
Evelyn
Evelyne
Evelynn
Evelynne
Evening
Ever
Everallin
Everest
Everett
Everild
Everine
Everita
Everle
Everlee
Everleigh
Everley
Everlie
Everly
Everlynn
Evermoore
Evermore
Evernie
Evette
Evey
Evgenia
Evgenija
Evia
Eviana
Evianna
Evie
Evienne
Eviris
Evis
Evita
Evniki
Evolet
Evon
Evonne

Evony
Evora
Evvie
Evy
Evyenia
Ewa
Ewelina
Exene
Exie
Eyre
Ezra
Ezri

F

Fabiana
Fabienne
Fabiola
Fabrizia
Fae
Faedra
Faël
Faelynn
Fahima
Faidra
Faiga
Faigel
Faiqa
Fairamay
Fairlie
Fairlight
Fairuza
Fairy
Faith
Faithful
Faiza
Fajga
Fala
Faline
Fallon
Fallyn
Falon

Famke
Fannie
Fanny
Fantasia
Fantine
Fara
Farah
Fareena
Faria
Farida
Faridah
Farin
Farishta
Farlyn
Farrah
Farren
Farrow
Farwah
Faryn
Fate
Fatima
Fatma
Fatoumata
Faun
Fausta
Faustina
Faustine
Fawn
Fawne
Fay
Faya
Faye
Fayla
Faylee
Fayrah
Fayth
Faythe
Fe
Fearne
Feather
Febe
February
Federica
Fedora
Feigel
Felecia

Felesha
Felice
Felicia
Feliciana
Felicidad
Felicita
Felicitas
Felicite
Felicitti
Felicity
Felienne
Felina
Felipa
Felisa
Felisha
Felixa
Feliz
Felizia
Femke
Femma
Fenella
Fenisia
Fenna
Fenris
Feodora
Feodosia
Ferdinando
Ferelith
Fermina
Fern
Fernanda
Fernande
Ferne
Ferre
Ferrin
Feyre
Ffion
Fflur
Fia
Fiadh
Fiala
Fiamma
Fiammetta
Fianna
Fidela
Fidelia

Fidelma
Fien
Fiera
Fifi
Filipa
Filippa
Filomena
Fina
Findabair
Finja
Finlay
Finleigh
Finley
Finna
Finnley
Finnula
Finola
Finula
Fion
Fiona
Fionna
Fionne
Fionnuala
Fiora
Fiore
Fiorela
Fiorella
Fiorenza
Fireese
Firenze
Flame
Flannery
Flavia
Flavie
Flechia
Flerida
Fleta
Fleur
Fleurette
Flicka
Fliss
Flo
Floor
Flor
Flora
Flòraidh

Florbela
Florence
Florencia
Florene
Florentina
Florentine
Floriana
Florice
Florida
Floride
Florimel
Florina
Florinda
Florine
Florrie
Flossie
Floy
Flutura
Flynn
Fonda
Forever
Fortuna
Fortunata
Fortune
Fotini
Fotoula
Foxglove
Fraida
Fran
Franca
France
Francelle
Frances
Francesca
Franchesca
Francheska
Francia
Francie
Francille
Francina
Francine
Francis
Francisca
Franciszka
Francoise
Frania

Franka
Frankie
Franklinia
Frannie
Franny
Franya
Franziska
Frauke
Fraya
Fred
Freda
Freddie
Frederica
Frèdèrique
Fredricka
Freeda
Freedom
Freelove
Freema
Freida
Freja
Frenchy
Freya
Freyda
Freyde
Freyja
Frida
Friday
Frideriki
Frieda
Frith
Frona
Frostine
Fulvia

G

Gabby
Gabi
Gable
Gabourey
Gabrianna
Gabriel
Gabriela
Gabriele
Gabriella
Gabrielle
Gabrriella
Gabryella
Gaby
Gaea
Gael
Gaela
Gaelen
Gaelle
Gaelyn
Gaetana
Gaia
Gail
Gaila
Gailey
Gailyn
Gaja
Gala

Galadriel
Galatea
Galaxie
Galaxy
Gale
Galen
Galena
Galene
Galia
Galiana
Galicia
Galilahi
Galilani
Galilea
Galilee
Galina
Galit
Gallifrey
Gamora
Gamze
Gaoge
Garance
Garbo
Garcelle
Garden
Gardenia
Garland
Garner
Garnet
Garnett
Garnette
Garrady
Garrison
Gates
Gatha
Gavi
Gavriela
Gavriella
Gay
Gayatri
Gaye
Gayla
Gayle
Gaylyn
Gaylynn
Gaynell

Gaynor
Gearldine
Geena
Geertruida
Geeta
Gela
Gelain
Geline
Gelsey
Gelsomina
Gem
Gema
Gemma
Gena
Genaine
Genavee
Genavieve
Gene
Genece
Genesee
Genesia
Genesis
Geneva
Genevie
Genevieve
Geneviva
Genevive
Genevra
Genie
Genifer
Genise
Gennifer
Genny
Gennyfer
Genova
Genovefa
Genoveffa
Genoveva
Genowefa
Genta
Gentry
Genvieve
George
Georgeanne
Georgene
Georgeta

Georgette
Georgia
Georgiana
Georgianna
Georgianne
Georgie
Georgina
Georgine
Geovana
Geraldean
Geraldina
Geraldine
Geralyn
Gerarda
Gerd
Gerda
Gergana
Geri
Germaine
Gerri
Gerrianne
Gerry
Gersende
Gertie
Gertrude
Gertrudis
Gesine
Gessica
Gevvie
Ghia
Ghislaine
Ghufran
Gia
Giachetta
Giacinta
Giacoma
Giacomina
Giada
Giana
Gianella
Gianetta
Gianina
Gianna
Giannah
Giannetta
Giannina

Giavanna
Gidget
Gift
Gigi
Gila
Gilberta
Gilda
Gilia
Gillian
Gilly
Gilma
Gina
Ginette
Ginevra
Ginger
Ginna
Ginnie
Ginnifer
Ginny
Gioacchina
Gioconda
Gioia
Giordana
Giorgia
Giorgina
Giovanna
Gisela
Gisele
Gisella
Giselle
Gisselle
Gitana
Gitel
Gitte
Gittel
Giuditta
Giulia
Giuliana
Giulianna
Giulietta
Giuseppa
Giuseppina
Giustina
Giverny
Gizelle
Gjertrud

Glada
Gladiola
Gladis
Gladus
Gladyce
Gladys
Gláucia
Glee
Glema
Glencora
Glenda
Glenna
Glennie
Glennis
Glimmer
Glinda
Gloria
Gloriana
Glorianne
Glorielle
Glory
Glow
Glynda
Glynis
Glynnis
Goda
Godelieve
Godiva
Gohlia
Golda
Golde
Golden
Goldia
Goldie
Goldy
Gomeisa
Goneril
Goretti
Graça
Grace
Gracealice
Gracee
Graceleigh
Gracella
Gracelyn
Gracelynn

Gracen
Gracey
Graci
Gracia
Graciana
Gracie
Graciela
Graciella
Gracionna
Gracyn
Grainne
Gramercy
Grania
Granuaile
Grasia
Gratia
Gratiana
Grauben
Gray
Grayce
Graycee
Graycen
Graycin
Graycn
Grayer
Graylin
Grayson
Grazia
Graziana
Graziella
Grażyna
Grear
Grecia
Greenlee
Greenley
Greer
Greetje
Gregoria
Greisy
Greta
Gretchen
Grete
Gretel
Grethe
Grey
Greylyn

Greysen
Greysi
Gricelda
Grier
Griet
Grigoria
Griselda
Griselle
Grizelle
Gro
Gruaidh
Gry
Guadalupe
Gudfrid
Gudrun
Guendalina
Guenevere
Guglielmina
Guillermin
Guillermina
Guin
Guinevere
Guinn
Gulielma
Gunhild
Gunn
Gunnhild
Gunvor
Gurbir
Gurdev
Guri
Gurleen
Gurmit
Guro
Gussie
Gusta
Guylaine
Gwen
Gwyn

H

Ha
  Habiba
  Hachi
  Haddie
  Haddy
  Haddyr
  Hadeel
  Hadiya
  Hadiyah
  Hadlee
  Hadleigh
  Hadley
  Hadlie
  Hadriana
  Haelee
  Haeley
  Haely
  Haf
  Hafsa
  Hafsah
  Hagar
  Haggith
  Haia
  Haidee
  Haidy
  Haidyn
  Haila

Haile
Hailee
Haileigh
Hailey
Haili
Hailie
Hailie-jade
Haily
Halcyon
Haldis
Halee
Haleigh
Halen
Haley
Hali
Halia
Halie
Halima
Halina
Halinor
Haliyah
Halle
Hallee
Halley
Halliday
Hallie
Halo
Halona
Halsey
Halyn
Hamest
Hamutal
Hana
Hanae
Hanah
Handan
Hande
Hania
Hanley
Hanna
Hannabella
Hannabelle
Hannah
Hannah-Mae
Hannalee
Hannalore

Hanne
Hanneli
Hannelore
Hannie
Happy
Hara
Hardeep
Hardial
Hareena
Harinder
Haris
Harjinder
Harlean
Harlee
Harleigh
Harlene
Harleth
Harley
Harli
Harlie
Harlow
Harlowe
Harlyn
Harmoni
Harmonia
Harmonie
Harmony
Harolyn
Harper
Harpreet
Harriet
Harriett
Harriette
Hartley
Haruhi
Haruka
Haruko
Harvest
Harvind
Hasia
Hasmig
Hasmik
Hassana
Hassie
Hatisha
Hatsuko

Hatsumomo
Hattie
Hatty
Hava
Havana
Havannah
Haven
Haverly
Havilah
Havily
Haviva
Hawa
Hawise
Haya
Hayastan
Hayat
Haydee
Hayden
Haydyn
Hayelee
Hayes
Hayla
Haylee
Haylei
Hayleigh
Hayley
Hayli
Haylie
Hazel
Hazeline
Hazelle
Hazle
Heather
Heaven
Heavenly
Hebe
Hedda
Hedra
Hedvig
Hedwig
Hedy
Heela
Hege
Heghine
Heidi
Heidy

Heike
Heila
Heini
Hejsa
Helaina
Helaine
Heledd
Heleena
Heleentje
Helen
Helena
Helene
Helewise
Helga
Helia
Heliodora
Helle
Hellen
Helma
Helmi
Heloise
Helori
Helsinki
Helyn
Hema
Hena
Hend
Hendrika
Henny
Henria
Henrienna
Henrietta
Henriette
Henryka
Hensley
Hephzibah
Hepzibah
Hera
Herkash
Herlinda
Herlinde
Hermelinda
Hermia
Hermila
Hermina
Hermine

Herminia
Hermione
Hermosa
Hero
Hersilia
Herta
Hertha
Hesper
Hessie
Hester
Hestia
Hettie
Hetty
Hiba
Hila
Hilaria
Hilarie
Hilary
Hilda
Hilde
Hildegard
Hildegarde
Hildegunn
Hildie
Hildred
Hildur
Hildy
Hilla
Hillari
Hillary
Hilma
Himawari
Hina
Hinari
Hinata
Hind
Hinda
Hinkley
Hinlee
Hiro
Hiromi
Hiwot
Hjördís
Hjørdis
Hoda
Hode

Holiday
Holland
Holley
Holli
Holliday
Hollie
Hollin
Hollis
Hollison
Holliston
Holly
Hollyann
Hollyn
Honalei
Honesty
Honey
Honor
Honora
Honorata
Honorée
Honoria
Honorine
Hope
Hopelyn
Horatia
Hortencia
Hortense
Hortensia
Hosanna
Hotaru
Houston
Hrieya
Hristina
Hrystyna
Hudson
Hue
Hulda
Huldah
Huma
Humaira
Hunter
Huyana
Hye
Hypatia

I

Ianna
    Iantha
    Iara
    Iavora
    Iben
    Ibis
    Ibiza
    Ibolya
    Iceley
    Icelyn
    Ichene
    Iciar
    Icie
    Icy
    Ida
    Idabel
    Idabelle
    Idalia
    Idalina
    Idalis
    Idalys
    Idawilla
    Ideane
    Idele
    Idelene
    Idelette
    Idell

Idella
Idina
Idit
Idolina
Idonia
Idony
Idra
Idun
Iesha
Ieva
Iezabel
Ife
Ifeoma
Ifrah
Iga
Ignacia
Igora
Igraine
Iida
Iiris
Ila
Ilah
Ilaia
Ilana
Ilanah
Ilar
Ilaria
Ilda
Ilde
Ildiko
Ilean
Ileana
Ileane
Ilee
Ileen
Ilene
Ilenia
Iley
Ilham
Ilia
Iliana
Iliar
Ililar
Ilithyia
Illiana
Illona

Illyana
Illyria
Ilona
Ilsa
Ilsamae
Ilse
Iluka
Ily
Ilyra
Ilyse
Ilysia
Ilyssa
Ilythia
Ima
Imagine
Iman
Imani
Imari
Imelda
Imnas
Imogen
Imogene
Imola
Impi
Ina
Inaara
Inanna
Inara
Inarah
Inaya
Inbal
Independence
India
Indiana
Indiasa
Indica
Indie
Indigo
Indira
Indra
Indy
Indya
Ine
Ineka
Inell
Ines

Inesh
Ineska
Inessa
Inez
Inga
Inge
Ingebjørg
Ingeborg
Inger
Ingjerd
Ingrid
Ingunn
Ingvild
Iniki
Inira
Inka
Inmaculada
Inna
Innogen
Ino
Inocencia
Inona
Insa
Inslee
Insuaf
Intisar
Invicta
Io
Ioana
Ioanna
Iola
Iolanda
Iolanta
Iolanthe
Iole
Iona
Ione
Ionela
Ionia
Iosefini
Iosifina
Ioulia
Iouliana
Ioulietta
Iounia
Ioustini

Iowa
Iphigenia
Ira
Iracema
Iraina
Irasema
Irati
Ireana
Ireland
Irelee
Irely
Irelyn
Irelynn
Irem
Iren
Irena
Irene
Iresine
Iria
Iridessa
Irie
Irina
Irini
Iris
Irisa
Irja
Irma
Irmegard
Irmgarde
Irmhild
Iro
Irulan
Isa
Isabeau
Isabel
Isabela
Isabeli
Isabelina
Isabell
Isabella
Isabelle
Isabelline
Isabeth
Isabetta
Isadora
Isalia

Isaline
Isamar
Isannah
Isaura
Isaure
Isavella
Iscah
Iseabail
Isela
Iselda
Iselin
Iselle
Iselyn
Iset
Iseult
Isha
Ishani
Ishara
Ishbel
Ishmel
Isidora
Isioma
Isis
Isla
Islay
Isledith
Islene
Islette
Isley
Islyn
Ismae
Ismay
Ismene
Ismeni
Ismerai
Ismeria
Ísmey
Ismini
Isobel
Isobella
Isobelle
Isola
Isolde
Isolene
Isolina
Isolyn

Isora
Isotta
Isqesia
Isra
Israa
Israel
Israella
Issa
Issabella
Istra
Isy
Itala
Italia
Italiah
Italy
Itati
Itsuki
Itzal
Itzayana
Itzel
Itzia
Iuile
Iulia
Iuliana
Iustina
Iva
Ivah
Ivaleine
Ivalo
Ivalyce
Ivana
Ivani
Ivanka
Ivanna
Iveigh
Ivelisse
Ivette
Ivona
Ivonne
Ivory
Ivy
Ivyna
Iwona
Ixchel
Ixia
Ixora

Iya
Iyana
Iyanna
Iyla
Iysabel
Izabel
Izabela
Izabella
Izabelle
Izabett
Izaskun
Izell
Izetta
Iziane
Izusa
Iúile

J

Jabre
Jacalyn
Jacee
Jacelyn
Jacelynn
Jacey
Jacie-Ann
Jacinda
Jacinta
Jacintha
Jacinthe
Jackeline
Jackelyn
Jackie
Jackleen
Jacklyn
Jacklynn
Jackquelin
Jaclyn
Jacoba
Jacobina
Jacolyn
Jacomina
Jacqi
Jacque
Jacquelin
Jacquette

Jacqui
Jacquline
Jacqulyn
Jacy
Jacyn
Jacynda
Jacynthe
Jada
Jadagrace
Jadalyn
Jade
Jadelyn
Jaden
Jadeyn
Jadie
Jadis
Jadranka
Jadrian
Jadwiga
Jadyn
Jadzia
Jaede
Jaedyn
Jaedynne
Jael
Jaeleigh
Jaelie
Jaelle
Jaelyn
Jaelynn
Jaffa
Jagger
Jagoda
Jagtar
Jahdiel
Jahnavi
Jahniya
Jahzara
Jaibrian
Jaice
Jaida
Jaidan
Jaide
Jaiden
Jaidin
Jaidyn

Jailand
Jailyn
Jaima
Jaimah
Jaimarie
Jaime
Jaimee
Jaimi
Jaimie
Jaina
Jaisa
Jakayla
Jakita
Jaklena
Jalana
Jalandra
Jalanea
Jaleesa
Jaleigh
Jalisa
Jalissa
Jaliyah
Jalyn
Jalynn
Jamaica
Jamariyah
Jamelle
James
Jamesina
Jameya
Jami
Jamia
Jamie
Jamie-Lynn
Jamieson
Jamila
Jamilah
Jamina
Jamison
Jamisyn
Jamiya
Jamiyah
Jammie
Jamya
Jamye
Jamyn

Jan
Jana
Janada
Janae
Janai
Janaia
Janaliz
Janana
Janay
Janaya
Janaye
Jancey
Janda
Jane
Janea
Janean
Janeane
Janeen
Janel
Janell
Janella
Janelle
Janene
Janeska
Janessa
Janet
Janeth
Janette
Janey
Janiah
Janice
Janie
Janiece
Janiela
Janina
Janine
Janiqua
Janis
Janisa
Janita
Janiya
Janiyah
Jann
Janna
Jannah
Janne

Janneane
Janneke
Jannelle
Jannette
Janney
Jannicke
Jannie
Jannika
Janny
Jansen
Janson
January
Janyce
Japera
Japji
Jaqlyn
Jaquelin
Jaqueline
Jara
Jardena
Jarielle
Jarima
Jaroslawa
Jaryn
Jasayla
Jasbinder
Jasbir
Jasdhir
Jaselle
Jasey
Jasika
Jasilyn
Jasinta
Jasleen
Jaslene
Jaslyn
Jasmer
Jasmijn
Jasmin
Jasmina
Jasminah
Jasmine
Jasmyn
Jasmynn
Jasneha
Jasperine

Jassy
Jasvir
Jatae
Jataunia
Jauslyn
Javiera
Jaxyn
Jaya
Jaycee
Jaycie
Jayda
Jaydah
Jayde
Jayden
Jaydyn
Jayella
Jayelle
Jayla
Jaylah
Jaylee
Jayleen
Jayleesa
Jaylen
Jaylene
Jayli
Jaylie
Jaylin
Jaylyn
Jaylynn
Jayma
Jayme
Jaymee
Jaymi
Jayna
Jayne
Jaynella
Jaysona
Jaz
Jazelle
Jazlene
Jazlin
Jazlyn
Jazlynn
Jazmin
Jazmine
Jazmyn

Jazmyne
Jazz
Jazzelle
Jazzlyn
Jazzlynn
Jazzmin
Jazzmyn
Jazzmyne
Jazzy
Jean
Jeana
Jeane
Jeanene
Jeanette
Jeanie
Jeanine
Jeanlee
Jeanna
Jeanne
Jeannette
Jeannie
Jeannine
Jeannique
Jeanyne
Jedda
Jeffyne
Jefri
Jehanne
Jehona
Jekka
Jelena
Jelia
Jelina
Jelisaveta
Jelise
Jelissa
Jemarica
Jemi
Jemima
Jemina
Jemma
Jemmy
Jen
Jena
Jenae
Jenalie

Jenalynn
Jenava
Jenavie
Jenavieve
Jenay
Jenaye
Jence
Jendra
Jenean
Jeneane
Jenecee
Jenée
Jenell
Jenelle
Jenessa
Jenettia
Jeneva
Jenevieve
Jeni
Jenianna
Jenibeth
Jenica
Jenice
Jenicka
Jenifer
Jenifry
Jenilee
Jenilyn
Jenine
Jenivee
Jenji
Jenn
Jenna
Jennabelle
Jenne
Jennea
Jennefer
Jenni
Jennica
Jennie
Jennifer
Jennika
Jennilie
Jennipher
Jennsen
Jenny

Jenoah
Jensen
Jensey
Jensine
Jensyn
Jensynn
Jentrie
Jentzie
Jenya
Jeraldine
Jereza
Jeri
Jerica
Jerilyn
Jerin
Jerline
Jerri
Jerrica
Jerrie
Jerry
Jersey
Jerusha
Jeryl
Jeselle
Jesenia
Jesica
Jesika
Jeslyn
Jesminder
Jesmyn
Jesmynda
Jess
Jessa
Jessah
Jessaly
Jessalyn
Jessalynn
Jessame
Jessamine
Jessamy
Jessamyn
Jessany
Jesse
Jessemy
Jessenia
Jessi

Jessica
Jessicah
Jessie
Jessika
Jessilyn
Jessique
Jesslyn
Jessyca
Jessye
Jessyka
Jestina
Jesus
Jesusa
Jesy
Jetta
Jette
Jettie
Jewel
Jewelia
Jewelianne
Jewell
Jexi
Jeyne
Jezabel
Jezabelle
Jezebel
Jezelle
Jezmine
Jezra
Jhené
Jhenna
Jia
Jiana
Jianne
Jifinder
Jill
Jillaine
Jillana
Jillene
Jillian
Jilliana
Jillianne
Jillyn
Jimena
Jimilia
Jimmie

Jina
Jing
Jinger
Jinia
Jinjer
Jinny
Jinora
Jinsy
Jiraiya
Jisinia
Jitka
Jiya
Jizelle
Jlynn
Jo
Joah
Joaida
Joan
Joana
Joanie
Joaninha
Joann
Joanna
Joanne
Joannie
Joaquina
Jobyna
Jocasta
Joceline
Jocely
Jocelyn
Jocelyne
Jocelynn
Jochebed
Jocleta
Joclyn
Jodee
Jodelle
Jodette
Jodi
Jodie
Jody
Joe
Joela
Joelea
Joelene

Joella
Joelle
Joellen
Joellyn
Joely
Joene
Joesette
Joetta
Joey
Johana
Johanna
Johannah
Johanne
Johari
Johna
Johnette
Johnie
Johnna
Johnnie
Johnny
Joi
Joie
Joisy
Joiya
Jojo
Jolaife
Jolan
Jolana
Jolanda
Jolanta
Jolee
Joleen
Joleigh
Jolene
Jolette
Jolie
Jolina
Joline
Jolisa
Jolynn
Jomana
Jóna
Jonatha
Jonbenet
Jonda
Jondy

Jonelle
Jonet
Joni
Joni leah
Jonina
Jonna
Jonni
Jonnie
Jonquil
Jonty
Jora
Jorah
Jorality
Jordan
Jordana
Jordanka
Jordanna
Jordanne
Jordenne
Jordie
Jordin
Jordy
Jordyn
Jordynn
Jorelle
Joretta
Jorga
Jorgia
Jori
Jorid
Jorie
Jorine
Jorja
Jorjiana
Jorlin
Jorun
Jorunn
Josafina
Josalina
Josaly
Josalyn
Josannah
Joscelin
Joscelyn
Josée
Josefa

Josefiina
Josefin
Josefina
Josefine
Joselda
Joselin
Joseline
Joselyn
Josepha
Josephina
Josephine
Josette
Joshie
Josia
Josiane
Josie
Josielle
Joslin
Joslyn
Joss
Josseline
Josselyn
Jossie
Josslyn
Josslynn
Joule
Jourdain
Jourdan
Jourden
Journee
Journey
Jovana
Jovanna
Jovano
Jovie
Jovienne
Jovita
Joy
Joy Anna
Joya
Joyann
Joyanna
Joyce
Joycelyn
Joye
Joyelle

Joylynn
Joyzelle
Jozefa
Jozefien
Jozefin
Juana
Juanev
Juanita
Jubilee
Jude
Judee
Judi
Judie
Judit
Judita
Judite
Judith
Judy
Juinita
Jula
Julee
Juleigha
Julene
Julep
Jules
Juli
Julia
Julia-Louise
Juliana
Juliane
Juliani
Juliann
Julianna
Julianne
Julie
Juliea
Julieann
Julieanne
Julienna
Julienne
Juliet
Julieta
Julieth
Julietta
Juliette
Julija

Julina
Julisa
Juliska
Julissa
Julita
Julitta
Juliza
Jullie
July
Julyana
Juna
June
Juneau
Junella
Junette
Juni
Junia
Junie
Junifa
Juniper
Juno
Jupiter
Jurgita
Jurnee
Justice
Justina
Justine
Juul

K

Kaawa
Kabibe
Kabira
Kacey
Kachina
Kaci
Kacibrel
Kacie
Kacy
Kadejah
Kaden
Kadence
Kadesha
Kadie
Kadience
Kadin
Kadison
Kady
Kadyn
Kadynce
Kaede
Kaeden
Kaedy
Kaedyn
Kaegan
Kaela
Kaelah

Kaeleigh
Kaeley
Kaeli
Kaelia
Kaelie
Kaelin
Kaely
Kaelyn
Kaelynn
Kaelynne
Kaena
Kagome
Kahealani
Kahlan
Kahlen
Kahli
Kahlia
Kahlika
Kahlila
Kahlo
Kahnay
Kai
Kaia
Kaiah
Kaiala
Kaianna
Kaida
Kaidee
Kaidence
Kaidyn
Kaie
Kaija
Kaila
Kailah
Kailani
Kaile
Kailea
Kaileah
Kailee
Kaileena
Kaileigh
Kailey
Kailia
Kailin
Kailla
Kaille

Kaillie
Kaily
Kailyn
Kailynn
Kailynne
Kaimee
Kainalu
Kairah
Kairi
Kairy
Kaisa
Kaisee
Kaisley
Kait
Kaiti
Kaitlen
Kaitlin
Kaitlyn
Kaitlyne
Kaitlynn
Kaitlynne
Kaitrin
Kaity
Kaiulani
Kaiva
Kaiya
Kaiye
Kaizer
Kaja
Kajsa
Kakalina
Kako
Kala
Kalani
Kalasin
Kalea
Kalee
Kaleena
Kaleia
Kaleigh
Kalena
Kalene
Kalera
Kalere
Kaley
Kali

Kalia
Kaliana
Kalie
Kalika
Kalila
Kalilah
Kalimba
Kalina
Kalinda
Kaliope
Kalissa
Kalista
Kalita
Kaliyah
Kallan
Kalli
Kallie
Kalliniki
Kalliope
Kalliopi
Kallista
Kallisto
Kally
Kallysta
Kalmia
Kaltun
Kalyani
Kalyca
Kalyn
Kalynda
Kalynn
Kalynne
Kalysta
Kama
Kamala
Kamalei
Kamara
Kamari
Kamaria
Kamaya
Kamaye
Kamber
Kambree
Kambri
Kambrie
Kamdyn

Kamea
Kameron
Kameryn
Kami
Kamia
Kamila
Kamilah
Kamilė
Kamilia
Kamilla
Kamille
Kamlyn
Kamma
Kammie
Kamora
Kamri
Kamrie
Kamry
Kamryn
Kamrynn
Kamya
Kamyra
Kana
Kanani
Kanata
Kanchan
Kandace
Kandi
Kandice
Kandie
Kandis
Kandra
Kandy
Kandyhn
Kanella
Kani
Kanika
Kaniqua
Kannon
Kansas
Kanupriya
Kanya
Kaori
Kaprinta
Kara
Karah

Karalee
Karalina
Karalyn
Karamia
Karan
Karanne
Karcey
Kareema
Kareen
Kareena
Karel
Karen
Karena
Karenna
Karesa
Karessa
Kari
Karianne
Karidee
Karie
Karigan
Karilynn
Karime
Karin
Karina
Karine
Karis
Karisa
Karishma
Karisma
Karissa
Karita
Karitas
Karla
Karlan
Karlee
Karleigh
Karlene
Karley
Karli
Karliah
Karlie
Karling
Karlotta
Karly
Karlyn

Karlyssa
Karma
Karmala
Karmen
Karmil
Karna
Karol
Karola
Karolin
Karolina
Karoline
Karolyn
Karon
Karou
Karren
Karri
Karrie
Karrigan
Karrington
Karris
Karrisa
Karryghan
Karstyn
Karsyn
Karter
Karuna
Kary
Karyme
Karyn
Karyna
Karyssa
Kasandra
Kasanita
Kasey
Kasha
Kashi
Kasia
Kasie
Kasmira
Kassady
Kassah
Kassandra
Kassi
Kassia
Kassidy
Kassie

Kassioni
Kassity
Kassy
Kastyn
Kasumi
Kat
Kata
Katala
Katalia
Katalin
Katalina
Katalyn
Katana
Katania
Katara
Katariina
Katarina
Katarine
Kataryna
Katarzyna
Katchen
Kate
Katelin
Katell
Katelya
Katelyn
Katelynn
Katelynne
Katenka
Kateri
Katerin
Katerina
Katerine
Katey
Kathaleen
Katharina
Katharine
Katharyn
Katherin
Katherina
Katherine
Katheryn
Katheryne
Kathi
Kathia
Kathie

Kathiria
Kathleen
Kathlyn
Kathrina
Kathrine
Kathryn
Kathryne
Kathy
Kathyria
Kati
Katia
Katiana
Katianna
Katie
Katilyn
Katilynn
Katin
Katina
Katinka
Katiya
Katja
Katla
Katlin
Katlina
Katlyn
Katlynn
Katniss
Katoria
Katra
Katrena
Katresa
Katri
Katriane
Katrianna
Katrice
Katriel
Katrien
Katriina
Katrijn
Katrin
Katrina
Katrine
Katrinka
Katsa
Katsiaryna
Kattie

Katy
Katya
Katyann
Katyna
Kavelle
Kaveri
Kavita
Kavya
Kay
Kaya
Kayah
Kayce
Kaycee
Kaycie
Kayda
Kaydee
Kayden
Kaydence
Kaydra
Kaye
Kayla
Kaylah
Kaylan
Kaylana
Kaylani
Kaylea
Kaylee
Kayleen
Kayleigh
Kaylen
Kaylene
Kayley
Kayli
Kayliana
Kaylianne
Kaylie
Kayliegh
Kaylin
Kayloni
Kaylor
Kaylyn
Kaylynn
Kaylynne
Kayna
Kayra
Kayse

Kaysi
Kaysie
Kaytlin
Kazandra
Kaziah
Kazimiera
Kazzandra
Ke$ha
Ke' Ondra
Kea
Keala
Kealia
Kealoha
Keana
Keani
Keara
Kearson
Keatley
Keatlyn
Keavy
Kecia
Keda
Kedma
Keeah
Keegan
Keela
Keeley
Keelia
Keelin
Keely
Keelyn
Keena
Keeria
Keersten
Keesha
Keeva
Keeyush
Kehau
Keheley
Keiani
Keiara
Keighan
Keighley
Keiko
Keila
Keilah

Keilani
Keilani Sky
Keilee
Keily
Keimy
Keira
Keiralee
Keirsta
Keiryn
Keisha
Keishla
Keisy
Keitha
Kejanae
Kekepania
Kekilia
Kelani
Kelby
Kelcee
Kelcey
Kelci
Kelcie
Kelda
Keleigh
Kelendria
Kelenna
Keli
Kelia
Keliah
Kelina
Kelis
Keliyah
Kellee
Kelleen
Kelleigh
Kellene
Keller
Kellesha
Kelley
Kelli
Kelli-ann
Kellianne
Kellie
Kellii
Kellina
Kelly

Kelly-Marie
Kellyanne
Kellyn
Kelsa
Kelsea
Kelsee
Kelsey
Kelsi
Kelsie
Kelsy
Kelti
Keltie
Kely
Kelyn
Kemelly
Kemery
Kenadee
Kenadie
Kenda
Kendahl
Kendal
Kendall
Kendalle
Kendell
Kendra
Kendrix
Kendy
Kendyl
Kendyleigh
Kendyll
Kenede
Kenia
Kenlee
Kenley
Kenlyn
Kenna
Kennadi
Kennadie
Kennady
Kennedi
Kennedy
Kennera
Kennette
Kennis
Kensa
Kensington

Kensley
Kentley
Kenya
Kenyada
Kenyatta
Kenza
Kenzie
Kenzington
Kenzinton
Kenzlie
Keomi
Keona
Kera
Keren
Kerensa
Kerenza
Keri
Kerianne
Kerin
Kerisa
Kerishia
Kerison
Kerith
Kerli
Kerlisia
Kerra
Kerri
Kerria
Kerriann
Kerrie
Kerrigan
Kerrin
Kerrirose
Kerrstin
Kerry
Kerryn
Kerstin
Kerstina
Kertle
Kerttu
Kesari
Kesha
Keshia
Kesiah
Kesley
Kesli

Keslyn
Kessie
Kessla
Kesslee
Kesslie
Kessly
Kestrel
Ketevan
Ketina
Kettra
Ketura
Keturah
Ketzalli
Keva
Keyara
Keyla
Keyna
Keyne
Keyona
Kezeah
Kezia
Keziah
Kezya
Kezziah
Khadeeja
Khadejah
Khadija
Khadijah
Khaleesi
Khalela
Khalfanee'
Khali
Khalida
Kharisma
Kharlia
Kharlie
Kharlotte
Khataleya
Khawla
Khe'Anna
Khera
Kherington
Khia
Khloe
Khloee
Khloei

Kholoud
Khora
Khoza
Khristian
Khristina
Khya
Khyany
Kia
Kiah
Kiana
Kianna
Kianne
Kiara
Kiarelys
Kiarn
Kiarra
Kiava
Kiba
Kida
Kidada
Kiela
Kiele
Kielle
Kiely
Kiera
Kierah
Kieran
Kiernan
Kierra
Kierslei
Kierslyn
Kiersten
Kierstyn
Kieryn
Kiffany
Kiira
Kiirah
Kika
Kiki
Kiko
Kiku
Kiley
Kilmeny
Kim
Kima
Kimba

Kimber
Kimberlee
Kimberleigh
Kimberley
Kimberli
Kimberlin
Kimberly
Kimberlyn
Kimberlynn
Kimbra
Kimery
Kimika
Kimiko
Kimimila
Kimisha
Kimm
Kimmie
Kimmy
Kimonia
Kimora
Kimya
Kina
Kindle
Kindness
Kindra
Kine
Kineret
Kinga
Kingsleigh
Kingsley
Kinlee
Kinley
Kinnery
Kinnia
Kinnor
Kinsey
Kinslee
Kinsley
Kinvara
Kinza
Kinzey
Kinzie
Kinzy
Kioka
Kiona
Kiowa

Kira
Kiralescense
Kiran
Kirby
Kirci
Kiri
Kiriana
Kirjah
Kirke
Kirov
Kirpa
Kirra
Kirrali
Kirralie
Kirrea
Kirrilie
Kirrily
Kirryn
Kirsa
Kirsi
Kirsie
Kirsta
Kirstal
Kirsten
Kirsti
Kirstie
Kirstin
Kirsty
Kirstyn
Kisha
Kismet
Kistine
Kit
Kitana
Kitarni
Kitianna
Kitiara
Kitka
Kittie
Kitty
Kitzi
Kiva
Kivrin
Kiwa
Kiya
Kiyrah

Kizzie
Kizzy
Kjellaug
Kjersti
Kjerstin
Klaire
Klara
Klarisa
Klarissa
Klarys
Klaudia
Klaudie
Klaudija
Klavdija
Klavdiya
Klea
Kleo
Kloe
Kloey
Klymene
Knarik
Knightley
Knox
Kobe
Kodi
Kodie
Koharu
Koi
Kojii
Kolbie
Kolby
Koleta
Kolette
Kolynn
Komal
Konnie
Konstantina
Konstantine
Kooper
Kora
Koral
Koralia
Korbyn
Kordae
Kore
Koree

Koren
Korena
Korene
Kori
Koribella
Korie
Korina
Korinna
Korinne
Kornelia
Korra
Korrelia
Korrie
Korrina
Kortnee
Kortney
Kortni
Korva
Kosi
Kostandea
Koti
Kourtlynn
Kourtney
Kourtnie
Kovie
Kree
Kreine
Kreszentia
Krichia
Krina
Kris
Krisentha
Krisha
Krishna
Krissi
Krissy
Krista
Kristal
Kristan
Kristeen
Kristel
Kristelle
Kristen
Kristi
Kristia
Kristian

Kristiana
Kristiania
Kristie
Kristiina
Kristin
Kristina
Kristine
Kristle
Kristol
Kristy
Kristyn
Kristyna
Krisztina
Kriti
Krizia
Krosbie
Krysia
Kryska
Krysta
Krystal
Krystallo
Krysten
Krystin
Krystina
Krystine
Krystle
Krystyna
Ksenia
Ksenija
Kseniya
Ksenya
Kuljit
Kulwant
Kulwinder
Kumi
Kura
Kwanza
Kwyn
Ky-Asia
Kya
Kyah
Kyanne
Kyara
Kyelei
Kyelle
Kyilea

Kyla
Kylah
Kylar
Kyle
Kylea
Kylee
Kyleena
Kyleigh
Kylene
Kyler
Kyley
Kyli
Kylia
Kylie
Kylin
Kyline
Kylise
Kylyne
Kylynn
Kymbre
Kymmy
Kyna
Kynlee
Kynley
Kynnley
Kynthia
Kynzlee
Kyoko
Kyra

L

Laasya
Labonita
Lacey
Lachlyn
Laci
Lacia
Lacie
Lacinda
Lacine
Lacona
Laconia
Lacy
Ladeca
Ladina
Ladonna
Ladora
Lady
Laekyn
Lael
Laela
Laelia
Laeticia
Laetitia
Lagertha
Lai
Laia
Laigh

Laika
Laiken
Laiklyn
Laikyn
Laila
Lailah
Lailani
Lailee
Laina
Laine
Laineigh
Lainey
Lainie
Laisha
Lake
Lakeisha
Lakelyn
Lakelynn
Laken
Lakenn
LaKenya
Lakesha
Lakeshia
Lakey
Lakin
Lakisha
Lakken
Lakota
Lakshmi
Lakyn
Lala
Lalacia
Lalaine
Lale
Lalia
Lalita
Lama
Lamai
Lameeha
Lamese
LaMia
Lamis
Lana
Lanah
Lanaya
Landel

Landly
Landree
Landrey
Landrie
Landry
Landy
Lane
Lanette
Laney
Langley
Langston
Lani
Lanie
Lanier
Lanis
Lanisa
Laniyah
Lanna
Lannaya
Lannie
Lanre
Lantana
Laoise
Lapis
Laquisha
Laquita
Lara
Larah
Laraine
Laralie
Laramie
LaRay
Laree
Lareina
Larelie
Laren
Lariah
Larina
Larique
Laris
Larisa
Larissa
Lark
Larkin
Larkspur
LaRonda

Larose
Larsen
Larue
Larysa
Laryssa
LaSalle
Lashae
Lashanda
Lashawn
LaShaye
Lashonda
Lassen
Lassie
Latanya
Latasha
Lateshia
Latetia
Lathria
Laticia
Latifa
Latika
Latikah
Latisha
Latitia
Latonia
Latonya
Latosha
LaToya
Latrice
Latricia
Lauden
Laudina
Laura
Laurah
Lauraine
Lauralee
Lauralin
Lauralynn
Lauran
Laurana
Lauranne
Laurayne
Laure
Laureen
Laurel
Laurelai

Laureline
Lauren
Laurena
Laurence
Laurenda
Laurene
Laurentia
Laurentien
Laurentine
Lauretta
Laurette
Lauri
Lauriana
Lauriane
Laurianna
Laurianne
Laurie
Lauriel
Laurina
Laurine
Lauryn
Lavada
LaVaughan
Lavender
Lavenia
Lavera
Lavergne
Lavern
Laverna
Laverne
Laveta
Lavian
Lavina
Lavinah
Lavinia
Lavon
Lavonda
Lavonne
Lawanda
Laxmi
Layali
Layce
Layla
Laylah
Layle
Laylee

Laylon
Layloni
Laylynn
Layna
Layne
Laynie
Layton
Lazeena
Lazuli
Le'nique
Lea
Leafaudo
Leah
Leahanna
Leahla
Leahona
Leala
Lealand
Leana
Leandra
Leane
Leann
Leanna
Leanne
Leanor
Leanora
Lear
Leatha
Leatrice
Leda
Ledisi
Ledora
Ledoux
Lee
Lee Ann
Leeann
Leeanne
Leeba
Leela
Leelah
Leelo
LeeLou
Leen
Leena
Leeonna
Leesa

Leeya
Leeza
LeFae
Legacy
Legna
Lehanna
Leia
Leialoha
Leida
Leigh
Leigh Ann
Leigh-Anne
Leigha
Leighann
Leighanna
Leighdyn
Leighla
Leighsaide
Leighton
Leila
Leilah
Leilana
Leilani
Leilia
Leilyn
Leina
Leisa
Leisel
Leisha
Leisl
Leitis
Lejla
Lela
Lelah
Leletia
Lelia
Leliana
Lelly
Lemma
Lemon
Lempi
Lena
Lenai
Lenaila
Lencha
Lene

Lenée
Leni
Lenina
Lenka
Lenke
Lenna
Lennan
Lennie
Lennika
Lennis
Lennon
Lennox
Lenora
Lenore
Lenox
Lenuța
Leo
Leoba
Leocadia
Leokadia
Leola
Leoma
Leomi
Leon
Leona
Leonarda
Leone
Leonela
Leonia
Léonie
Leonila
Leonor
Leonora
Leonore
Leontina
Leontine
Leor
Leora
Leoris
Leota
Leotie
Lera
LeRae
Lerin
Lerina
Lerusha

Lesa
Lesage
Lesedi
Lesia
Leslee
Lesley
Lesli
Lesliana
Leslie
Lesly
Leslye
Lessa
Lessia
Lessie
Leta
Letha
Leticia
Letitia
Letizia
Leto
Lettice
Lettie
Letty
Levana
Leven
Levenez
Levi
Levina
Levius
Levonica
Levy
Lex
Lexa
Lexee
Lexi
Lexie
Lexine
Lexington
Lexus
Lexy
Lexzandra
Leyah
Leyanna
Leydi
Leyila
Leyla

Leylani
Leymah
Leyna
Leyton
Lezah
Lezlie
Lhotse
Li
Li Li
Lia
Liadain
Liadan
Liadawn
Lian
Liana
Liane
Lianna
Lianne
Liara
Liat
Liath
Liba
Libba
Libbe
Libbie
Libby
Libelle
Liberata
Liberta
Libertad
Liberty
Libitina
Libiya
Liboria
Licha
Licia
Lida
Liddie
Liddy
Lidewei
Lidewij
Lidia
Lidian
Lidiann
Lidija
Lidiya

Lidmila
Liduvina
Lidwina
Lidya
Lieke
Lielle
Lien
Lienna
Lierin
Liesbeth
Liesel
Lieselotte
Liesl
Lieve
Lif
Ligaya
Ligeia
Ligia
Lihi
Liisa
Lil
Lila
Lilac
Lilah
Lilaina
Líle
Lileas
Lileigh
Lili
Lilia
Lilian
Liliana
Liliane
Lilianna
Lilianne
Lilias
Lilibet
Lilibeth
Lilidh
Lilien
Lilienne
Lilika
Lilike
Liliosa
Lilit
Lilita

Lilith
Lilium
Liliwen
Liliya
Lilja
Liljana
Lill
Lilla
Lillah
Lillemor
Lilli
Lillia
Lilliah
Lillian
Lilliana
Lilliandil
Lilliann
Lillianna
Lillianne
Lillibet
Lillie
Lilliella
Lillienna
Lillienne
Lillith
Lilly
Lilly-may
Lillyana
Lilo
Lilou
Lily
Lilyan
Lilyana
Lilyanna
Lilyanne
Lilybelle
Limor
Lin
Lina
Lincy
Lind
Linda
Linden
Lindie
Lindley
Lindsay

Lindsey
Lindsie
Lindsy
Lindy
Line
Lineke
Linet
Linette
Linh
Linit
Linleigh
Linley
Linn
Linnae
Linnaea
Linnea
Linnet
Linnete
Linnie
Linny
Linnzi
Linor
Linoy
Linsay
Linsey
Linza
Linzee
Linzey
Linzi
Lio
Lioba
Lionella
Lionese
Lior
Liora
Liori
Liorit
Lirael
Lirah
Liraz
Liriel
Lirit
Lisa
Lisa Ann
Lisa-Marie
Lisabeth

LisaJo
Lisalla
Lisandra
Lisanne
Lisbet
Lisbeth
Lise
Liselle
Liselotte
Liseth
Lisette
Lisha
Lisieli
Lisle
Lismely
Lissa
Lissandra
Lisse
Lissette
Lissianna
Lissie
Lissy
Lita
Litzy
Liv
Liva
Livana
Live
Livia
Livian
Liviana
Livianna
Livienne
Livier
Livija
Liviya
Livna
Livvy
Livy
Liya
Liyah
Liz
Liza
Lizabeth
Lizanne
Lizbeth

Lizelle
Lizeth
Lizette
Lizzet
Lizzette
Lizzie
Lizzy
Ljuba
Ljubica
Ljudmila
Lleucu
Llewella
Lluvia
Lobelia
Lockie
Locklyn
Loen
Logan
Loida
Loïe
Loire
Lois
Lola
Loleta
Lolita
Lollia
Lollie
Lolly
Loma
Lona
Londa
Londen
London
Londyn
Lone
Lonette
Loni
Lonie
Lonika
Lonna
Lonnie
Loorea
Lora
Lorah
Loraine
Loral

Loralai
Loralei
Loralie
Loralye
Loranda
Lorca
Lore
Lorea
Loredana
Loreen
Loreena
Lorelai
Lorelei
Loreley
Lorelii
Lorella
Lorelotte
Loren
Lorena
Lorenda
Lorene
Lorenza
Loreto
Loretta
Lorette
Lori
Lorial
Lorian
Loriana
Loriann
Lorianne
Lorie
Lórien
Lorine
Lorisha
Lorissa
Lorna
Lorraine
Lorrein
Lorri
Lorrie
Losana
Lotta
Lotte
Lotti
Lottie

Lotus
Lou
Louann
Louanne
Loucia
Louela
Louella
Louelle
Louetta
Louie
Louisa
Louise
Louisiana
Louisine
Loukia
Loukritia
Loulabelle
Loulah
Louna
Loura
Lourdes
Louressa
Louvenia
Lova
Love
Loveday
Loveena
Lovely
Lovelyn
Lovepreet
Lovetta
Lovette
Lovey
Lovice
Lovie
Loviisa
Lovina
Lovisa
Lowanna
Lowena
Lowenna
Lowery
Lowri
Loxie
Loxley
Loyce

Loys
Lu
Lua
Luan
Luana
Luann
Luanna
Luanne
Luba
Lubalethu
Lubna
Lubomira
Luca
Lucasta
Luce
Lucea
Lucee
Lucelly
Lucero
Lucetta
Lucette
Lucey
Lucia
Luciah
Luciana
Lucianne
Lucie
Lucienne
Lucija
Lucila
Lucile
Lucilia
Lucilla
Lucille
Lucina
Lucinda
Lucine
Lucja
Lucky
Lucrece
Lucrecia
Lucretia
Lucrezia
Lucy
Ludema
Ludie

Ludivine
Ludmila
Ludmilla
Ludovica
Lue
Luela
Luella
Luellen
Luellyn
Luetta
Lugenia
Luigia
Luigina
Luisa
Luisana
Luise
Luisina
Luisne
Luiza
Luizianna
Lujing
Luka
Lula
Lulamae
Lulana
Lular
Lulette
Lulie
Lulu
Lumay
Lumen
Lumex
Lumi
Luna
Lunah
Lunanina
Lundy
Lune
Lunette
Lupe
Lupica
Lupine
Lupita
Lura
Luree
Luria

Lurlene
Lurline
Lusia
Lusine
Lutessa
Lúthien
Lutie
Luvenia
Luvia
Luvianna
Luvinia
Lux
Luxe
Luxi
Luz
Luza
Luzetta
Luzi
Luziana
Luzviminda
Lyanna
Lyda
Lydia
Lydian
Lydie
Lygia
Lykke
Lyla
Lylah
Lylia
Lyliann
Lylliann
Lyn
Lynae
Lynda
Lyndee
Lynden
Lyndi
Lyndsay
Lyndsey
Lyndsie
Lynee
Lynelle
Lyness
Lynette
Lynlea

Lynlee
Lynley
Lynn
Lynnae
Lynne
Lynnea
LynneAnne
Lynnelle
Lynnette
Lynnezi
Lynnie
Lynnix
Lynnzi
Lynnzie
Lynsey
Lynsi
Lynsy
Lynx
Lynzee
Lyonelle
Lyra
Lyri
Lyria
Lyric
Lyrik
Lyris
Lysandra
Lysanne
Lysithea
Lyska
Lyssa
Lyssie
Lystra
Lyta

M

Maaria
Maaike
Maartje
Maaskelah
Maayan
Mabel
Mabelle
Mabilia
Mable
Mabley
Mabrey
Mabrie
Mabry
Mabyn
Macala
Macara
Macarena
Macaria
Macayla
Macee
Macey
Machelle
Machion
Maci
Macie
Mackan
Macyn

Mada
Madailein
Madalena
Madalie
Madalina
Madaline
Madalitso
Madalyn
Madalyne
Madalynn
Maddalena
Maddalina
Madden
Maddie
Maddison
Maddox
Maddy
Maddyn
Maddysun
Madeira
Madelaina
Madelaine
Madelca
Madelein
Madeleine
Madelen
Madelena
Madeleva
Madelief
Madeline
Madelon
Madelyn
Madelynn
Madelynne
Madge
Madhavi
Madhuri
Madi
Madicella
Madicken
Madie
Madigan
Madiha
Madilyn
Madilynn
Madisen

Madison
Madisyn
Madja
Madlen
Madleyne
Madonna
Madrid
Madrigal
Mady
Madylan
Madylin
Madyn
Madysen
Madyson
Mae
Maebel
Maebh
Maebress
Maebry
Maeby
Maecy
Maedhbh
Maegan
Maegen
Maeghan
Maeleigh
Maeliana
Maelie
Maelle
Maëlly
Maelona
Maelyn
Maelynn
Maëlys
Maeoni
Maerin
Maeryn
Maesen
Maesie
Maeva
Maeve
Maeven
Maevyn
Maewyn
Maezie
Mafalda

Magali
Magalie
Magaly
Maganda
Magda
Magdalen
Magdalena
Magdalene
Magdalini
Magdalone
Magdalyn
Magdeline
Magdilyn
Magdolna
Magenta
Maggie
Magna
Magnhild
Magnolia
Mago
Maha
Mahala
Mahalath
Mahaley
Mahalia
Maham
Mahdis
Mahgan
Mahi
Mahleah
Mahogany
Mahra
Mahri
Mahsa
Mahtab
Mai
Maia
Maiah
Maiara
Maicean
Maida
Maiden
Maïder
Maigen
Maija
Maika

Maike
Maiken
Maila
Maile
Mailee
Maille
Mailyn
Mair
Maira
Maire
Mairead
Mairi
Máirín
Mairwen
Maisey
Maisha
Maisica
Maisie
Maison
Maissa
Maisy
Maisyn
Maite
Maitreya
Maivelyn
Maiwen
Maiwenn
Maiya
Maizey
Maizie
Maizy
Maja
Majandra
Majda
Majella
Majerle
Majken
Majlinda
Majlis
Makada
Makaela
Makaila
Makailyn
Makaira
Makala
Makali

Makaya
Makayla
Makaylah
Makaylee
Makeady
Makeda
Makena
Makenlee
Makenna
Makenzi
Makenzie
Makhyden
Makia
Makinley
MaKinzi
Makiya
Makynzie
Malaak
Malaika
Malainie
Malak
Malala
Malamatenia
Malana
Malani
Malarie
Malaya
Malayka
Malayna
Malaysia
Malea
Maleah
Maleigha
Malena
Malene
Malerie
Målfrid
Malgorzata
Malia
Maliah
Maliana
Malie
Maliha
Malika
Malin
Malina

Malinda
Malion
Malisa
Malise
Malissa
Maliyah
Malka
Mallaidh
Mallie
Mallika
Mallori
Mallorie
Mallory
Malon
Maloree
Malorie
Malory
Malou
Malva
Malvern
Malvina
Malwina
Malysa
Mamaine
Mame
Mameha
Mamie
Mammie
Manacca
Manami
Manar
Manda
Mandala
Mandalay
Mandalit
Mandana
Mandi
Mandie
Mandy
Manervia
Manhattan
Manini
Manisha
Manita
Manja
Manjit

Manju
Manjula
Manney
Manon
Manoritha
Manpreet
Mansi
Manuela
Manuella
Manya
Maple
Mar
Mara
Marabel
Marabella
Marabelle
Marabeth
Marable
Maraed
Marah
Marais
Marajade
Maraleigh
Maralyn
Marama
Maran
Maranda
Maranzie
Marbella
Marca
Marcail
Marcela
Marcelina
Marceline
Marcella
Marcelle
Marcelline
Marchel
Marcheline
Marchelle
Marchesa
Marci
Marcia
Marcie
Marciella
Marcy

Mardelle
Mardi
Mardie
Maree
Mareesa
Mareesha
Mareille
Mareisa
Marel
Marelaine
Marely
Maren
Maret
Mareta
Mareva
Marga
Margaery
Margaid
Margalit
Margalo
Margaret
Margareta
Margarete
Margareth
Margaretha
Margarethe
Margarett
Margaretta
Margarette
Margarida
Margarita
Margaux
Marge
Margeaux
Marged
Margene
Margery
Margherita
Margi
Margie
Margit
Margo
Margot
Margret
Margreta
Margy

Marharyta
Mari
Maria
Maria Jose
Mariah
Mariajose
Marialena
Mariam
Mariama
Mariamne
Marian
Mariana
Marianel
Marianela
Mariangela
Mariann
Marianna
Marianne
Marianthi
Mariasha
Maribel
Maribella
Maribelle
Maribeth
Marica
Maricarmen
Maricela
Maricia
Mariclare
Maricris
Maricza
Marie
Marie-Ange
Marie-Claire
Marie-Emmanuelle
Marie-Ève
Marie-France
Marie-Josée
Marieke
Mariel
Mariela
Mariele
Marielena
Mariella
Marielle
Mariely

Mariena
Marienna
Marieta
Marietta
Mariette
Marifel
Marifrances
Marigny
Marigold
Marigoldita
Marigot
Marija
Marijana
Marijka
Marijke
Marika
Mariko
Marilee
Marilena
Marilene
Marilla
Marilou
Marilu
Marilyn
Marilynn
Marilynne
Marin
Marina
Marinana
Marinda
Marine
Marinea
Marinela
Marinella
Marinelle
Marinika
Marinn
Marion
Marionna
Mariot
Mariposa
Maris
Marisa
Marisah
Marisela
Marisen

Marisha
Marishka
Mariska
Marisol
Marissa
Maristella
Marit
Marita
Marites
Maritess
Marith
Maritza
Mariya
Mariyah
Mariza
Marja
Marjane
Marjanna
Marjolaine
Marjolein
Marjorie
Marjory
Markella
Marketa
Marketta
Markie
Markisha
Markita
Marla
Marlaina
Marlaine
Marlana
Marlayna
Marlee
Marleen
Marleigh
Marlen
Marlena
Marlene
Marlenie
Marlett
Marley
Marleyna
Marli
Marlia
Marliana

Marlie
Marline
Marlis
Marlise
Marlo
Marloes
Marlow
Marlowe
Marly
Marlyn
Marlys
Marmar
Marna
Marnetta
Marnette
Marney
Marni
Marnica
Marnie
Marny
Marolyn
Marquita
Marre
Marretje
Marryn
Marsaili
Marsali
Marseille
Marsha
Marsia
Marta
Marte
Martel
Martha
Marthann
Marthe
Marthy
Marti
Martina
Martine
Martinique
Martita
Martta
Marty
Martyna
Marusia

Maruxa
Marva
Marvel
Marvelous
Marvina
Marwa
Mary
Mary Ann
Maryam
Maryann
Maryanna
Maryanne
Marybelle
Marybeth
Maryella
Maryelle
Maryellen
Marygrace
Maryjane
Maryjo
Marykay
Marylal
Marylee
Marylin
Marylou
Marylyn
Maryn
Maryrose
Marysa
Maryse
Maryssa
MarySue
Maryte
Marzena
Marzia
Masada
Masae
Masako
Masani
Maselyn
Masha
Masie
Masika
Maslyn
Mason
Massie

Massiel
Masumi
Masyn
Mataline
Mataya
Matea
Matel
Matema
Mathea
Mathilda
Mathilde
Matia
Matiana
Matiese
Matilda
Matilde
Matilija
Matilyn
Matina
Matisse
Matleena
Matlin
Matsey
Mattea
Matthea
Mattie
Maty
Matylda
Matyleen
Maud
Maude
Maudeen
Maudie
Mauilena
Maura
Maureen
Maurica
Mauricia
Maurine
Mauve
Mava
Maven
Mavis
Mavra
Max
Maxene

Maxie
Maxima
Maximina
Maximum
Maxine
May
Maya
Mayada
Mayah
Mayan
Mayar
Mayara
Maybell
Maybelle
Maybelline
Maycee
Maye
Mayela
Mayella
Mayim
Mayla
Maylea
Maylee
Mayleigh
Maylene
Mayley
Maylin
Maylis
Mayme
Maymie
Mayra
Maysan
Maysen
Mayson
Mayte
Mayuri
Mayzee
Mayzelle
Mayzie
Mazal
Mazarine
Mazel
Maziah
Mazie
Mazzy
Mckella

Mckenna
Mclean
Mea
Meabh
Meadhbh
Meadow
Meagan
Meagen
Meaghan
Meara
Méav
Mecca
Meche
Mechelle
Meda
Medb
Medbh
Medea
Medeleine
Medha
Medhani
Medhya
Media
Medina
Medora
Medusa
Meegan
Meegyn
Meena
Meera
Meesa
Meeta
Meg
Megaera
Megan
Megane
Megara
Megève
Meggan
Meggie
Meggin
Meghan
Meghann
Meghna
Meghyn
Megumi

Megyn
Mehetabel
Mehitabel
Mehitable
Mehnoush
Mehri
Mei
Mei Ling
Meidhbhin
Meifeng
Meighan
Meika
Meike
Meilani
Meilin
Meinir
Meinwen
Meira
Meirit
Meissa
Meja
Mekanna
Mekeda
Mel
Mela
Meladi
Melaina
Melaine
Melana
Melane
Melanee
Melania
Melanie
Melanija
Melantha
Melantho
Melany
Melanya
Melba
Melda
Mele
Meleah
Melek
Melena
Melenna
Melia

Meliah
Melian
Meliauna
Melika
Melike
Melina
Melinda
Meline
Meliora
Melisa
Melisande
Melisandre
Melisha
Melissa
Melissza
Melita
Melitta
Meliz
Mellear
Mellesse
Mellie
Mellisa
Mellissa
Mellyn
Melodean
Melodee
Melodie
Melody
Melonie
Melony
Melora
Melpomene
Melrose
Melusine
Melva
Melvina
Melvyne
Melyna
Melynda
Melyndra
Melyor
Melyssa
Mem
Memory
Memphis
Mena

Menaka
Menali
Mendian
Mendy
Menka
Menodora
Menolly
Meranda
Merav
Merced
Mercedes
Mercier
Mercy
Meredith
Merel
Merete
Merethe
Merey
Meri
Meriam
Meribeth
Merida
Meridel
Meridian
Meridith
Meriel
Merilyn
Merindah
Meris
Merissa
Merit
Meritt
Merle
Merlene
Merna
Merope
Meropi
Merralina
Merran
Merriann
Merrick
Merridan
Merrie
Merrigan
Merrilee
Merrilyn

Merritt
Merry
Merryn
Mersades
Mersey
Mersia
Mertie
Merula
Merveille
Meryl
Mesa
Mesche'
Meschelle
Mesila
Mestra
Meta
Metha
Metrodora
Metta
Mette
Metzli
Meya
Meyrick
Mhairi
Mhya
Mia
Miabella
Miah
Miata
Mica
Micaela
Micah
Micarla
Micayla
Micha
Michael
Michaela
Michaele
Michaeline
Michaella
Michaelle
Michaila
Michal
Michala
Michalina
Michaya

Michayla
Michela
Michele
Michelette
Michelina
Micheline
Michell
Michella
Michelle
Michellette
Michiko
Michon
Michonne
Miciah
Miciela
Mickayla
Mickey
Micki
Mickie
Midajah
Midge
Midori
Mie
Mieke
Mieko
Miel
Mielle
Miesha
Mietta
Miette
Migdalia
Miglė
Mignon
Mihaela
Mihr
Miigan
Mika
Mikaela
Mikaelah
Mikah
Mikaila
Mikako
Mikala
Mikalyn
Mikan
Mikasa

Mikaya
Mikayla
Mikaylee
Mikelle
Mikenna
Mikenzi
Mikenzie
Mikhaila
Mikki
Miku
Mila
Milabelle
Milada
Milagros
Milan
Milana
Milani
Milania
Milaslava
Milcah
Mildred
Mildrid
Milena
Miley
Mili
Miliani
Milica
Mililani
Milissa
Milja
Milla
Millaray
Millay
Mille
Miller
Milliana
Millianna
Millican
Millicent
Millie
Milligan
Milly
Milou
Mimi
Mimma
Mimmi

Mimsy
Min
Mina
Minami
Minda
Mindella
Mindelynn
Mindi
Mindl
Mindry
Mindy
Minea
Minelda
Minerva
Minette
Ming
Ming Yue
Minka
Minke
Minley
Minna
Minnie
Minta
Mintie
Minto
Minttu
Minty
Minuette
Minver
Miosoti
Miquela
Miquella
Miquita
Mira
Mirabai
Mirabel
Mirabella
Mirabelle
Miracle
Mirah
Mirai
Mirain
Mirana
Miranda
Mirasol
Miray

Mireia
Mireille
Mirel
Mirela
Mirele
Mirella
Mirena
Mireya
Miri
Miria
Miriam
Mirielle
Miriyana
Mirja
Mirjam
Mirlande
Mirna
Miroslava
Mirra
Mirren
Mirta
Mirth
Miryam
Misaki
Mischa
Misgana
Misha
Mishavonna
Mishelle
Mishon
Missie
Missouri
Missy
Misti
Misty
Mithian
Mittie
Mitzi
Mitzy
Miu
Miuccia
Miwa
Mixtlicoatl
Miya
Miyah
Miyu

Mizosuaniaka
Mizuki
Mlinda
Mlynn
Mo'Nesha
Moa
Moana
Modesta
Modesty
Moellyn
Moira
Moirrey
Molleigh
Molli
Mollie
Molly
Mollyann
Mona
Monaisha
Monalisa
Monet
Monica
Monifa
Monika
Monike
Monique
Monisa
Monna
Monnie
Monroe
Monserrat
Monserrate
Montana
Monterey
Montserrat
Monya
Moon
Moorea
Mopsie
Mora
Morag
Morana
Moray
Morena
Moressa
Morey

Morgaine
Morgan
Morgana
Morgane
Morgann
Morgause
Morgayne
Moria
Moriah
Moriko
Morinne
Morissa
Morna
Morning
Morrigan
Morrow
Morticia
Morven
Morwenna
Moscelyne
Moselle
Mosley
Mossie
Mostyn
Motley
Moumita
Mouna
Moxie
Moya
Mozell
Mozella
Mozelle
Mtima
Mudra
Muireann
Muirenn
Muirgheal
Muirne
Mulan
Muncie
Murasaki
Muriel
Muriella
Murphy
Murron
Muse

Musetta
Musidora
Mutiara
My
Mya
Myah
Myana
Myani
Myanthee
Myava
Mychelle
Myfanwy
Myhaley
Myka
Mykia
Myla
Mylah
Mylee
Myleene
Mylene
Mylie
Mystery

N

Naava
　Nabila
　Nabisa
　Nacole
　Nada
　Nadalie
　Nadalyn
　Nadalyne
　Nadasia
　Nadeen
　Nadejda
　Nadeleine
　Nadelle
　Nadia
　Nadie
　Nadina
　Nadine
　Nadira
　Nadiya
　Nadja
　Nadrine
　Nadya
　Nadylie
　Naevia
　Nahia
　Nahima
　Nahla

Nahlin
Nai'a
Naia
Naiara
Naida
Naila
Nailah
Naima
Nainsí
Naiomi
Naiya
Najya
Nakayla
Nakia
Nakira
Nakisha
Nakita
Nakusha
Nakushi
Nakya
Nala
Nalah
Nalani
Nalanie
Naléa
Naledi
Naleigh
Nalini
Nalla
Nalleli
Nallely
Namia
Namie
Naminé
Nan
Nana
Nanako
Nancee
Nancey
Nanci
Nancie
Nancy
Nandita
Nane
Nanea
Nanette

Nani
Nanina
Nanna
Nannerl
Nanneth
Nannette
Nannie
Nanrinder
Nantia
Nao
Naoimh
Naoise
Naoko
Naoma
Naome
Naomi
Naomie
Naomy
Naoual
Naousca
Naphtali
Nara
Narcisa
Narcissa
Nareh
Narelle
Nariah
Narina
Narinder
Narine
Narjis
Narscissa
Naserian
Nash
Nashya
Nasim
Nasra
Nasreen
Nasrine
Nassaria
Nastassia
Nastassja
Nastasya
Nastia
Nastya
Natacha

Natajia
Natalaya
Natalee
Nataleigh
Natali
Natalia
Natalie
Nataliee
Natalija
Natalina
Nataliya
Natalka
Nataly
Natalya
Natalyah
Natalyn
Natania
Natasa
Natascha
Natasha
Natasza
Nataszja
Natavia
Nateira
Nathalee
Nathalia
Nathalie
Nathaly
Nathanna
Natia
Natividad
Natosha
Natoya
Naushaba
Nausicaa
Nautica
Nava
Navdeep
Naveena
Navi
Navy
Nawal
Naya
Nayana
Nayara
Nayce

Nayeli
Nayelli
Nayely
Nayla
Nazanin
Nazareth
Nazayia
Nazeli
Nazlee
Nea
Neala
Necia
Necile
Necla
Neda
Nedeljka
Nedra
Neea
Neeka
Neeki
Neela
Neelam
Neelie
Neema
Neena
Neenagh
Neeru
Neesha
Neeta
Nefertari
Neferteri
Nefertiri
Neferure
Negar
Negin
Negina
Neha
Neida
Neila
Neina
Nekeia
Nekia
Nekisha
Neko
Nelda
Nele

Nelia
Neliah
Nelida
Nelinha
Nell
Nella
Nelle
Nelli
Nellia
Nellie
Nelly
Nelta
Nelwyn
Nemaiah
Nemain
Nemi
Nena
Neoma
Neona
Nephele
Nera
Neraida
Nerea
Nereida
Neri
Nerida
Nerilly
Nerine
Nerissa
Neroli
Nerys
Neshama
Nesita
Neslihan
Nessa
Nessarose
Nessie
Nesta
Neta
Netanya
Netta
Nettie
Nettle
Neva
Nevada
Nevaeh

Nevaeh Leigh
Nevanthi
Nevart
Neve
Neveah
Nevena
Neveyah
Neviana
Newlyn
Neysa
Neysha
Ngahuia
Ngaio
Ngaire
Ngairella
Ngozi
Nia
Niabi
Nialla
Niamara
Niamh
Niamha
Niana
Niara
Niawbrawaka
Niaz
Nicasia
Nichelle
Nichol
Nichole
Nicki
Nickie
Nickole
Nico
Nicola
Nicolasa
Nicole
Nicolene
Nicoleta
Nicoletta
Nicolette
Nicolien
Nicolina
Nicoline
Nicolle
Nida

Nidia
Niema
Niesha
Niesje
Nieva
Nieve
Nieves
Nigella
Nightingale
Nihad
Niharika
Nika
Nikaia
Nike
Nikeisha
Nikhazia
Niki
Nikia
Nikira
Nikita
Nikki
Nikkole
Nikohl
Nikol
Nikola
Nikole
Nikoleta
Nikolett
Nikolina
Nikoline
Nila
Nilah
Nilani
Nilda
Nile
Nilofer
Nilsa
Nimrat
Nimue
Nina
Ninel
Ninella
Ninette
Nineveh
Ninfa
Ninkasi

Nino
Ninon
Niobe
Niomi
Nionne
Niquole
Nira
NiRae
Niraimadhi
Nirali
Nirmala
Nirvana
Nisha
Nissa
Nita
Nitasha
Nitza
Nívea
Nixie
Niya
Niyla
Nneka
Noa
Noah
Noam
Nobuko
Noe
Noel
Noela
Noelani
Noeleta
Noelia
Noella
Noelle
Noely
Noemi
Noemia
Noémie
Nogah
Nohely
Nohemi
Noire
Nokomis
Nola
Nolia
Nollie

Nolwenn
Noma
Nombongo
Nomsa
Nomy
Nona
Nonie
Noomi
Noor
Noora
Nophar
Nora
Norah
Noralee
Noralyn
Norberta
Noreen
Noreena
Norella
Norellie
Norene
Norianna
Noriko
Norine
Norla
Norma
Normandy
North
Northa
Norunn
Noushin
Nova
Novah
Novalee
Novalie
Novara
Novasera
Novella
November
Novhina
Novi
Novia
Noya
Ntozake
Nuala
Nubia

Nuha
Nujood
Nunzia
Nunziatina
Nur
Nura
Nurani
Nuria
Nurit
Nver
Nya
Nyah
Nyaja
Nyala
Nyasia
Nydehlia
Nydia
Nyia
Nykia
Nyla
Nyomi

O

Oakes
Oaklee
Oaklynn
Oana
Obdulia
Ocean
Oceana
Ocie
Octavia
Octaviana
October
Oda
Odaliz
Odalys
Odalyz
Oddlaug
Oddny
Oddrun
Oddveig
Odelene
Odelia
Odell
Odessa
Odetta
Odette
Odie
Odile

Odilia
Odina
Odyssey
Ofeibea
Ofelia
Ofilia
Oghenerioborue
Ohana
Ohanna
Ohiyo
Oiva
Okaria
Okemia
Okera
Oki
Okimi
Oksana
Ola
Olaia
Olalla
Olamide
Olan
Olaug
Oldriska
Olena
Olene
Olesea
Oleta
Olethea
Olette
Olevia
Olga
Olia
Olidia
Olie
Olimpia
Olinda
Oline
Olinka
Oliva
Olive
Oliver.
Olivera
Olivette
Olivia
Oliviah

Oliviana
Olivié
Olivienne
Olivina
Olivine
Oliwia
Ollie
Olma
Olta
Oluyomi
Olwen
Olwyn
Olya
Olympia
Olympias
Olyssia
Olyvia
Oma
Omayra
Ombretta
Omie
Omolara
Ona
Onari
Onatah
Ondina
Ondine
Ondrea
Ondria
Onekka
Oneta
Ongela
Onie
Onika
Onnie
Onnika
Onora
Onycha
Onyx
Oona
Opal
Opaline
Ophelia
Ophélie
Ophellia
Ophia

Ophira
Oprah
Ora
Orabela
Orabella
Orah
Oraina
Oralia
Orazia
Orazio
Orchid
Orein
Oriana
Oriane
Orianna
Orianne
Orianthi
Orietta
Oriole
Orion
Orit
Orla
Orlagh
Orlain
Orlaith
Orlanda
Orlean
Orli
Orly
Ornella
Orpah
Orpha
Orquidea
Orsalina
Orsola
Orsolya
Ortensia
Orvalee
Osa
Osha
Osiana
Oska
Ossie
Ostara
Oswin
Otelia

Otha
Otilia
Ottaline
Ottavia
Ottie
Ottilia
Ottilie
Ottoline
Oudia
Ouida
Ourania
Oursoula
Ova
Ovelle
Owaissa
Owen
Owena
Owens
Oxana
Ozma

P

Pabla
Padma
Padmé
Padmini
Paetyn
Page
Paget
Pahi
Paige
Paigely
Paislee
Paisley
Paiton
Paityn
Paivi
Paizlie
Palapala
Pallas
Pallavi
Palma
Palmer
Palmira
Paloma
Pam
Pamala
Pamela
Pamella

Pamelyn
Pamina
Pamla
Pamposh
Panagiota
Panalin
Panchita
Pandora
Pangfua
Panjai
Panna
Pansie
Pansy
Paola
Paquita
Paradis
Paralee
Paramjit
Paraskevi
Parastoo
Pari
Parijaat
Paris
Parisa
Parker
Parminder
Parmjit
Parnel
Parthena
Parthenia
Parthenope
Parul
Parvana
Parvati
Parvin
Parys
Pascale
Pascaline
Paschal
Pascuala
Pasha
Paskalina
Pasqualina
Pasquina
Passion
Pat

Patience
Patina
Patrice
Patricia
Patrina
Patrisha
Patrizia
Patrycja
Patsey
Patsuqua
Patsy
Patta
Patti
Pattie
Patty
Paula
Pauletta
Paulette
Paulien
Paulina
Pauline
Paulita
Pavanne
Pavla
Pavlina
Pawandeep
Pawanjeet
Paxley
Paxton
Payne
Payson
Payten
Payton
Payzlee
Paz
Pazienza
Peace
Peach
Peaches
Pearl
Pearle
Pearlie
Pearline
Pearson
Pebbles
Peeri

Peg
Pegeen
Peggie
Peggy
Peighton
Pelagia
Pele
Pelia
Pella
Pema
Pemba
Pemma
Penda
Peneil
Penelope
Penina
Peninah
Peninnah
Penka
Penna
Penni
Pennie
Pennilyn
Pennington
Penny
Penrose
Peony
Pepa
Pepita
Pepper
Peppi
Perdita
Perenelle
Peri
Peridot
Perla
Perle
Permelia
Pernilla
Pernille
Perouze
Perpetua
Perri
Perrie
Perrine
Perry

Persayis
Persefoni
Persephone
Persia
Persimmon
Persis
Pervinca
Peryn
Peta
Petal
Petaline
Petra
Petrina
Petrita
Petronel
Petronella
Petronia
Petronila
Petronilla
Petrova
Petula
Petunia
Peyson
Peytin
Peyton
Peytyn
Phaedra
Phaelyn
Phaidra
Pheasant
Phebe
Phenyo
Phereby
Pheriche
Pheya
Philadelphia
Philippa
Philippina
Phillipa
Phillis
Philoma
Philomena
Philomene
Philyra
Phoebe
Phoenix

Photine
Phronsie
Phryne
Phylicia
Phylicity
Phylis
Phyllida
Phyllis
Pia
Pialy
Piatarihi
Picabo
Piedad
Pier
Piera
Pierina
Pieta
Pietja
Pietronella
Pihla
Pilar
Pina
Pinar
Pinelloppe
Pinelopi
Pinja
Pink
Pinkie
Pinky
Pinotta
Pip
Piper
Pippa
Pippi
Pire
Piri
Pita
Pixie
Pleasance
Pleasant
Plum
Pnina
Pocahontas
Poesia
Poesy
Poet

Poiema
Pola
Polaris
Polina
Polis
Polissena
Polliana
Pollie
Polly
Pollyanna
Polymnia
Polyxena
Pomeline
Pomona
Ponijao
Pooja
Poppi
Poppie
Poppy
Porsha
Portia
Portlyn
Posey
Posie
Posy
Potomac
Prabhpreet
Praema
Pragya
Prairie
Pranaya
Prarthana
Prascovia
Prashanti
Praskovya
Prathia
Praveena
Pravina
Precious
Preslee
Presley
Pressy
Prestyn
Pretoria
Prewitt
Pria

Prianna
Prim
Prima
Primavera
Primeveire
Primina
Primrose
Primula
Princess
Pris
Prisca
Priscila
Priscilla
Priscille
Priska
Priskilla
Prisma
Priya
Priyadarshini
Priyah
Priyanka
Promis
Promise
Puma

Q

Qamra
    Quanita
    Queenie
    Quenby
    Quentea
    Quentessa
    Querida
    Querube
    Queta
    Quetzal
    Quetzali
    Quetzalli
    Quiana
    Quillian
    Quincey
    Quincy
    Quindelia
    Quineta
    Quinlee
    Quinley
    Quinn
    Quinty
    Quirina

Rabia
Rachana
Racheal
Rachel
Rachele
Rachelle
Rachelyn
Rachyl
Racquel
Radha
Radhika
Radka
Radlee
Radomira
Rae
Rae-lynn
Raea
Raeann
Raeanne
Raechel
Raechelle
Raegan
Raeghan
Raeleah
Raelie
Raelin

Raelle
Raelyn
Raelyne
Raelynn
Raen
Raena
Raevynn
Raewyn
Rafaela
Rafaella
Raffaela
Raffaella
Raffia
Ragan
Ragna
Ragnhild
Rahel
Rahil
Rahima
Rahma
Rahne
Rain
Raina
Rainah
Rainbow
Raine
Rainey
Raini
Rainie
Rainn
Rainna
Rainy
Raisa
Raita
Raivyn
Raizel
Raja
Rajamani
Rajani
Rajika
Rajmund
Rakeidra
Rakel
Ralana
Raleigh

Raluca
Ramella
Ramelle
Ramey
Ramia
Ramiele
Ramjit
Ramona
Ramonita
Ramsi
Ramya
Rana
Randee
Randi
Randy
Ranee
Rani
Rania
Ranita
Ranjeet
Ranjir
Ranjit
Rannveig
Ranveig
Raphaela
Raphaëlle
Rapunzel
Raquel
Raquelle
Rasa
Rasha
Rashauna
Rasheeda
Rashel
Rashelle
Rashida
Rashmi
Rashpal
Ratchel
Ratnakara
Raumina
Rava
Raven
Ravenna
Ravinia

Raviva
Ravyn
Rawan
Ray
Raya
Rayah
Rayanna
Rayannah
Rayanne
Raychel
Rayelle
Rayen
Raygan
Rayla
Raylee
Rayleigh
Raylene
Rayliegh
Raylin
Rayme
Raymonde
Rayna
Rayne
Raynel
Raynne
Rayo
Rayquel
Rayssa
Rayven
Razaan
Razia
Razilee
Reagan
Reagen
Reanan
Reanna
Reatha
Reau
Reba
Rebbeca
Rebeca
Rebecca
Rebecka
Rebeckah
Rebeka

Rebekah
Rebekka
Rebel
Red
Redell
Reece
Reed
Reegan
Reem
Reema
Reena
Reese
Reeva
Reeve
Refugio
Regan
Regene
Reggie
Regina
Regine
Regitze
Rehema
Rehtaeh
Rei
Reia
Reid
Reidun
Reigh
Reighlynn
Reign
Reiley
Reilly
Réiltín
Reilynn
Reina
Reinette
Reisa
Rejoice
Rejoyce
Reka
Rekha
Rella
Rema
Remedios
Remember
Remenyi

Remi
Remilia
Reminisce
Remy
Remyah
Rena
Renae
Renata
Renate
Renatta
Rene
Renea
Renee
Renelle
Renesemee
Renesme
Renesmee
Reness
Reni
Renita
Renmani
Renna
Rennie
Renowe
Requiem
Resa
Resha
Reshma
Ressie
Reta
Retha
Retta
Reva
Reve
Reveka
Revekka
Revel
Reverie
Revital
Rexelle
Rey
Reyanne
Reyhan
Reyna
Reynae
Reynalda

Reynolds
Reza
Rhaine
Rhapsody
Rhayne
Rhea
Rheana
Rheanna
Rheanne
Rheba
Rhemi
Rheta
Rheyna
Rhian
Rhiane
Rhianna
Rhianne
Rhiannon
Rhianydd
Rhienne
Rhine
Rhiya
Rhoda
Rhona
Rhonda
Rhoswen
Rhosyn
Rhudi
Rhyan
Rhylan
Rhylee
Rhylen
Rhythm
Ría
Riahn
Rian
Riana
Riann
Rianna
Rianne
Riannon
Ricarda
Riccarda
Ricci
Richard
Richelle

Richie
Richmal
Rickelle
Rickie
Ricole
Ridgeley
Ridley
Rie
Riece
Riegan
Rieko
Rielle
Rielyn
Riesa
Riese
Rifka
Rifkah
Riga
Rigmor
Rihanna
Riho
Rika
Riki
Rikke
Rikki
Rikku
Riklynn
Riko
Rila
Rilda
Rilee
Rileigh
Riley
Rilla
Rilo
Rilynn
Rima
Rin
Rina
Rinah
Rini
Rinnah
Rinoa
Rinslet
Rio
Rioghnach

Riona
Rionach
Ripley
Risa
Risha
Rishita
Risica
Risika
Rita
Ritza
Riva
River
Riverlyn
Rivers
Riviera
Rivija
Rivka
Rivkah
Rivkie
Rixa
Riya
Rizpah
Roanne
Robbie
Robbin
Robbyn
Robert
Roberta
Robess
Robette
Robi
Robin
Robina
Roby
Robyn
Rochel
Rocheli
Rochelle
Rocío
Rocket
Rococo
Roelyn
Roena
Roenne
Roewyn
Rogue

Rohanna
Rohese
Rohini
Roisin
Roksana
Roksanaa
Rolanda
Rolande
Rolanna
Roma
Romaine
Romana
Romane
Romany
Rome
Romeeka
Romelia
Romelle
Romi
Romilda
Romilly
Romily
Romina
Romney
Romola
Romona
Romula
Romy
Rona
Ronaleah
Ronda
Ronette
Roni
Ronia
Ronit
Ronja
Ronke
Ronna
Ronni
Ronnie
Ronya
Roona
Rooney
Roos
Roosje
Rori

Rory
Rosa
Rosa Maria
Rosabel
Rosabella
Rosabelle
Rosabeth
Rosaelia
Rosaine
Rosalba
Rosaleah
Rosalee
Rosaleen
Rosaleigh
Rosalia
Rosalice
Rosalicia
Rosalie
Rosalina
Rosalind
Rosalinda
Rosaline
Rosalva
Rosalyn
Rosalynn
Rosamaria
Rosamel
Rosamond
Rosamund
Rosana
Rosangela
Rosangelica
Rosann
Rosanna
Rosannah
Rosanne
Rosaria
Rosario
Rosarja
Rosaura
Rose
Rose Marie
Rose-Anne
Rosealyn
Roseann
Roseanna

Roseanne
Rosebay
Rosebella
Roseen
Rosegunde
Rosel
Roselen
Roselet
Roselie
Roselin
Roselina
Roseline
Rosella
Roselma
Roselyn
Roselynn
Rosemarie
Rosemary
Rosemonde
Rosephanye
Roser
Roses
Rosetta
Rosette
Rosetti
Rosewillow
Rosewyn
Rosey
Roshni
Rosia
Rosianna
Rosica
Rosie
Rosilyn
Rosina
Rosita
Roslin
Roslyn
Roslynn
Rosmerta
Rossana
Rossella
Rossie
Rosslyn
Roswitha
Rosy

Rotem
Rouge
Roula
Rovetta
Rowan
Rowanna
Rowen
Rowena
Rowenna
Rowyn
Rowynn
Roxana
Roxane
Roxani
Roxann
Roxanna
Roxanne
Roxelana
Roxette
Roxia
Roxie
Roxolana
Roxy
Roya
Royal
Royalty
Royelle
Royse
Roza
Rozalija
Rozaliya
Rozalynn
Rozana
Rozanne
Rozella
Rozene
Rozenwyn
Rozi
Rozlyn
Rozlynn
Rozmari
Rozmin
Rozsika
Ruari
Ruathy
Rubaline

Rubi
Rubia
Rubianna
Rubicela
Rubie
Rubiela
Rubina
Ruby
Rubye
Ruchel
Rudy
Rue
Rufina
Ruhama
Ruhamah
Ruhi
Rumbidzai
Rumer
Rumina
Rumjana
Rumor
Runa
Rupinder
Rusalka
Ruslana
Russet
Rut
Ruta
Rute
Ruth
Ruthann
Ruthanna
Ruthanne
Ruthe
Ruthea
Ruthie
Ruthistle
Rutina
Ruxandra
Rya
Ryah
Ryan
Ryann
Ryanna
Ryanne
Rydel

Ryden
Ryder
Ryenne
Ryiah
Rylen

S

Saadia
Saadet
Saba
Sabah
Sabela
Sabella
Sabina
Sabine
Sabitha
Sable
Sabra
Sabriel
Sabrina
Sabrine
Sabriya
Sabry
Sacagawea
Saccha
Sacha
Sachi
Sachiko
Sacora
Sada
Sadako
Sadb
Sadbh
Sade

Sadhana
Sadhbh
Sadia
Sadie
Sadira
Sadiya
Sadye
Safaa
Saffi
Saffine
Saffron
Saffy
Safie
Safina
Safiya
Safra
Saga
Sagan
Sagas
Sage
Sager
Sagrario
Sahalie
Sahana
Sahar
Sahara
Saharud
Sahdiah
Sahra
Sahri
Saia
Saida
Saige
Saija
Saijal
Sailar
Sailor
Saina
Saira
Saiya
Sakai
Saki
Sakinah
Sakiya
Sakura
Sala

Saleisha
Salem
Salena
Saletta
Saliha
Salima
Salina
Salleigh
Sallie
Sally
Salma
Saloma
Salome
Salomea
Salomi
Saloomeh
Salud
Salustiana
Salustianna
Salvatrice
Salwa
Sam
Samai
Samaire
Samanda
Samanman
Samanta
Samantha
Samanvi
Samara
Samarah
Samaria
Sameera
Samhita
Samia
Samira
Samirah
Samiya
Samiyah
Sammi
Sammie
Samuella
Sana
Sanaa
Sanae
Sanai

Sanaya
Sanaz
Sancha
Sanchia
Sancia
Sandeep
Sandi
Sandie
Sandra
Sandriana
Sandrine
Sandy
Sang
Sangay
Sangeeta
Sanger
Sania
Saniah
Sanice
Saniya
Saniyah
Sanja
Sanjuana
Sanjuanita
Sanjukta
Sanna
Sannah
Sanne
Sanni
Sanra
Sansa
Santa
Santana
Santesa
Santidad
Santina
Santos
Sanura
Sanya
Saoirse
Saori
Saorla
Saorlaith
Saory
Sapana
Sapfo

Saphia
Saphira
Saphire
Saphyre
Sapna
Sapphira
Sapphire
Sappho
Sara
Sarabella
Sarabelle
Sarabeth
Sarabi
Sarabjit
Saradora
Sarafina
Sarah
Sarah-Jane
Sarahi
Sarai
Sarajane
Sarala
Saralyn
Saranda
Saraswati
Saray
Saraya
Sari
Saria
Sariah
Sarianne
Sarie
Sarielle
Sárika
Sarin
Sarina
Sarita
Sariyah
šárka
Sarnali
Saro
Sarojshree
Saron
Sarraly
Sarrauh
Sascha

Sasha
Sashi
Sashmir
Sashya
Saskia
Saskie
Sassa
Sassinak
Sati
Satiah
Satine
Satwant
Satya
Satyana
Saule
Saundra
Savana
Savanah
Savanha
Savanna
Savannah
Savayta
Savera
Savesti
Savina
Savine
Savira
Savita
Savoy
Savvy
Savy
Sawyer
Saya
Sayantani
Sayde
Saydee
Sayetsi
Sayli
Saylor
Sayre
Sayuri
Sayward
Sayyida
Scarlet
Scarlett
Scarletta

Scarlette
Scarlitt
Scarlytt
Scathach
Scholastica
Schuyler
Scilla
Scotia
Scotland
Scout
Sea
Seallie
Seana
Seanna
Season
Seaton
Seattle
Seawillow
Sebastiana
Sebastienne
Sebella
Sebrena
Secret
Sedef
Sedell
Sedna
Sedona
Sedora
Seema
Seersha
Seija
Seika
Seiko
Seimone
Seiren
Seisia
Sejal
Sela
Selah
Selby
Selena
Selenah
Selene
Selenia
Selenne
Selephia

Selia
Selie
Selin
Selina
Selinda
Selini
Sellene
Selma
Semele
Semelina
Semiha
Semira
Semiramis
Sena
Senaida
Senara
Senay
Seneca
Senfronia
Senga
Senja
Senna
Sennett
Sensia
Seo-yeon
Seona
Sephora
September
Septima
Sequoia
Sera
Serafina
Serah
Seraph
Seraphia
Seraphin
Seraphina
Seraphine
Sereana
Sereen
Sereia
Seren
Serena
Serenade
Serenah
Serendipity

Serene
Sereniah
Serenity
Seresa
Seretha
Serilda
Serina
Serinda
Serine
Serita
Seriyah
Serra
Sertab
Sesilia
Sessilee
Sethe
Setiya
Setota
Seva
Sevanne
Sevasti
Sevda
Sevde
Seven
Severa
Severena
Severina
Sévérine
Sevi
Sevilla
Sevina
Seychelle
Sha'uri
Shabnam
Shada
Shadi
Shadia
Shadiya
Shadyn
Shae
Shaela
Shaeleigh
Shaelie
Shaelyn
Shaelynn
Shaheen

Shahla
Shaianne
Shaielle
Shaienne
Shailene
Shailey
Shaina
Shaindel
Shakayla
Shakeh
Shakila
Shakira
Shakthi
Shakti
Shala
Shalanda
Shalica
Shalice
Shalimar
Shalina
Shalita
Shalom
Shalonda
Shalyn
Shamala
Shameka
Shamika
Shamiran
Shamiso
Shana
Shanae
Shanda
Shandi
Shandiin
Shandra
Shandrea
Shandy
Shane
Shanelle
Shanen
Shange
Shani
Shania
Shanice
Shanika
Shaniqua

Shanita
Shaniya
Shaniyah
Shanley
Shanna
Shannah
Shannan
Shannary
Shannelle
Shannen
Shannessy
Shannon
Shannondoeh
Shannyn
Shanon
Shanta
Shantae
Shante
Shantel
Shantell
Shantelle
Shanti
Shaquana
Shaquani
Shaquita
Shara
Sharalyn
Sharayah
Sharee
Shareen
Sharelle
Sharen
Sharena
Sharesa
Sharette
Shari
Sharice
Sharifa
Sharita
Sharkeisha
Sharla
Sharlee
Sharlene
Sharlie
Sharlotte
Sharman

Sharna
Sharnee
Sharon
Sharona
Sharonda
Sharpay
Sharron
Sharyn
Shashi
Shasta
Shatara
Shatavia
Shatha
Shauna
Shauni
Shaunice
Shaunna
Shaunteva
Shavon
Shavonne
Shawanda
Shawn
Shawna
Shawnee
Shawnie
Shawntae
Shawntelle
Shawree
Shay
Shayah
Shayda
Shayden
Shaye
Shayla
Shaylee
Shayleigh
Shaylene
Shaylie
Shaylin
Shaylyn
Shaylynn
Shayna
Shayne
Shea
Shealey
Shealyn

Shealynn
Sheba
Sheena
Sheethal
Sheherazade
Sheigh
Sheila
Sheindal
Sheine
Shekinah
Shelanda
Shelba
Shelbee
Shelbi
Shelbie
Shelby
Shelena
Shelene
Shelia
Shelice
Shelina
Shellcie
Shelley
Shelli
Shellie
Shelly
Sheloa
Shelton
Shelva
Shelyn
Shenae
Shenandoah
Shenequa
Shenoah
Sheraine
Sheralin
Sheree
Shereen
Sherelle
Sherene
Sheri
Sheridan
Sherie
Sherilyn
Sherin
Sherine

Sherita
Sherlee
Sherlyn
Sheron
Sherona
Sherra
Sherri
Sherrie
Sherrienna
Sherrill
Sherron
Sherry
Sherryl
Sherson
Sheryl
Shevaun
Shevit
Shey
Sheyenne
Sheyla
Shiane
Shianne
Shiela
Shifra
Shika
Shila
Shilah
Shillelagh
Shiloh
Shiniqua
Shinobu
Shiola
Shion
Shiphrah
Shira
Shiralee
Shiraz
Shireen
Shirella
Shirelle
Shirie
Shirin
Shirlee
Shirleen
Shirlene
Shirley

Shiva
Shivani
Shivi
Shiyel
Shlomit
Shohreh
Sholeh
Shoma
Shona
Shonda
Shonna
Shontelle
Shosanna
Shoshona
Shree
Shreenidhi
Shreeya
Shreya
Shrijani
Shriya
Shterna
Shula
Shulamit
Shulamith
Shura
Shushan
Shyamala
Shyann
Shyanna
Shyanne
Shyarna
Shyla
Shylah
Shylar
Shylee
Shylo
Shyloh
Shyly
Shytavia
Sia
Siahna
Sian
Siana
Siandrah
Sianna
Siara

Sibeal
Sibella
Sibilla
Sibley
Sibyl
Sibyll
Sibylla
Sibylle
Sicily
Siddalee
Siddaly
Siddha
Sidney
Sidonia
Sidonie
Sidony
Sidra
Sidsel
Sieana
Siella
Siena
Sienna
Siera
Sierra
Sierrah
Sif
Sigal
Sigfrida
Siglinda
Signe
Signy
Sigourney
Sigrid
Sigrun
Sigrunn
Sigurrós
Siham
Siiri
Sikwayi
Síle
Silena
Silence
Silene
Silje
Silka
Silke

Sille
Silvana
Silver
Silvia
Silviana
Silvie
Silvija
Sima
Simcha
Simi
Similkameen
Simona
Simone
Simonetta
Simonette
Simonida
Simonne
Simran
Simrin
Sina
Sinai
Sindhu
Sindi
Sine
Sinead
Sinforiana
Sini
Siobhan
Siobhana
Siofra
Siomha
Sionainn
Sionann
Siouxsie
Siran
Siranush
Siren
Sirena
Sirène
Siri
Siri.
Siriporn
Sirkka
Sirmata
Siroun
Sirvart

Sisely
Sissel
Sissela
Sissi
Sissy
Sister
Sistine
Sita
Sitara
Siuan
Siun
Siv
Sivan
Siwa
Siwan
Sixtine
Skadi
Skai
Skky
Sky
Skyden
Skye
Skyie
Skyla
Skylah
Skylan
Skylar
Skylark
Skyler
Skyli
Skylie
Skylynn
Skyrah
Slaina
Slava
Slavica
Slavka
Sloan
Sloane
Smera
Smilla
Smita
Smitha
Snefrid
Sneha
Snezhana

Snow
Snowelle
Snædís
Soazig
Socorra
Socorro
Soey
Sofia
Sofiah
Sofiana
Sofianne
Sofie
Sofija
Sofiya
Sofonisba
Sofy
Sofya
Soha
Sohalia
Sohnian
Sohvi
Soila
Sojourner
Sol
Sola
Solace
Solaina
Solana
Solange
Solara
Solaris
Solbjørg
Soledad
Soleil
Soleileia
Soleine
Solène
Solenne
Soleste
Sóley
Solfrid
Soliesse
Solita
Solja
Sollemnia
Solstice

Solveig
Solvej
Solvey
Soma
Somers
Sommer
Sona
Sonali
Sonaly
Sonary
Sonata
Sondra
Sonel
Song
Songkarn
Sonia
Sonja
Sonje
Sonnet
Sonoma
Sonora
Sonrisa
Sonya
Sookie
Sophea
Sopheah
Sopheia
Sophelia
Sophi
Sophia
Sophia Grace
Sophianne
Sophie
Sophie-Marie
Sophina
Sophonisba
Sophronia
Sophy
Soraia
Soraida
Sorana
Soraya
Soraya-rose
Sorcha
Sorella
Soriah

Sorina
Sorrel
Sorsha
Sose
Sosie
Sotiria
Soul
Sousanna
Souzanna
Sovannah
Sovay
Sovia
Sowenna
Sparks
Sparrow
Spencer
Spicer
Spring
Sreedevi
Stacey
Staci
Stacia
Stacie
Stacy
Stana
Stanislava
Star
Starla
Starleen
Starlene
Starley
Starli
Starlin
Starling
Starlynn
Starr
Stasia
Stasya
Stav
Stavroula
Steele
Stef
Stefani
Stefania
Stefanie
Steffany

Steffi
Stefka
Stela
Steliana
Stella
Stellabella
Stellar
Stellina
Stellita
Štěpánka
Steph
Stephani
Stephania
Stephanie
Stephany
Stephie
Stephy
Sterre
Stevie
Stina
Stine
Stiofáiín
Stojanka
Storie
Storm
Storme
Stormi
Stormie
Stormy
Story
Styliani
Støen
Su
Sudha
Sudie
Sue
Sue-Ann
Suellen
Sufiyah
Sugey
Suhaila
Suheily
Sujata
Sujatha
Sujey
Suka

Sukanya
Sukey
Suki
Sukie
Suky
Sula
Sule
Sulema
Sulia
Sulie
Sulochana
Sumaiya
Sumanjit
Sumaya
Sumayya
Sumiati
Sumire
Summah
Summer
Summiya
Sun
Sunako
Sundara
Sundari
Sunday
Sunflower
Sunita
Sunna
Sunni
Sunnie
Sunniva
Sunny
Sunrise
Sunset
Sunshine
Surabhi
Suranna
Suraya
Surelis
Suri
Surie
Surinder
Suriya
Surjeet
Surrey
Surriya

Sury
Surya
Susan
Susana
Susann
Susanna
Susannah
Susanne
Sushi
Sushila
Susie
Susy
Sutherlyn
Sutten
Sutton
Suuvi
Suvi
Suyana
Suzan
Suzana
Suzann
Suzanna
Suzannah
Suzanne
Suze
Suzette
Suzie
Suzy
Svanhild
Svea
Svetlana
Sveva
Swan
Swathi
Swati
Swayze
Sweta
Swintayla
Sy'rai
Syani
Sybella
Síle

T

Tabassum
Tabby
Tabetha
Tabia
Tabita
Tabitha
Tabrett
Tace
Tacey
Tacie
Tacita
Tacy
Taedra
Taeka
Taelyn
Taffeta
Taffryn
Taffy
Tagiane
Taguhi
Tahesha
Tahia
Tahira
Tahirih
Tahki
Tahlia
Tahliah

Tahlulah
Tahnee
Tai
Taide
Taige
Taija
Taika
Tailor
Tailynn
Taimi
Taina
Taisha
Taisie
Taissa
Taite
Taitlynn
Taitum
Taiya
Taja
Tajia
Tajinder
Takara
Tal
Talaina
Talaya
Taleah
Tali
Talia
Taliana
Talie
Talika
Talin
Talina
Talini
Talisa
Talise
Talitha
Taliyah
Talli
Tallis
Tallulah
Tally
Talmun
Talor
Talula
Talullah

Talya
Talyia
Talyn
Talynn
Talyse
Tamaira
Tamala
Tamaliah
Tamana
Tamar
Tamara
Tamarind
Tamaris
Tamaryn
Tamasin
Tamatha
Tambi
Tambria
Tameah
Tameka
Tamela
Tamera
Tamey
Tami
Tamia
Tamie
Tamika
Tamiko
Tamina
Tammi
Tammie
Tammiella
Tammin
Tammis
Tammy
Tamora
Tamra
Tamryn
Tamsen
Tamsie
Tamsin
Tamsyn
Tamura
Tamya
Tamzin
Tana

Tanae
Tanalyn
Tananda
Tanaya
Tanayah
Tancy
Tanda
Tandi
Tandilyn
Tanesha
Taney
Tangakin
Tangela
Tangier
Tangwystl
Tania
Tanika
Tanis
Tanisen
Tanisha
Tanit
Tanita
Tanith
Taniya
Taniyah
Tanja
Tanna
Tannar
Tanner
Tannis
Tansy
Tanya
Tanyka
Tanzie
Tara
Tara-Anjali
Tarah
Taraji
Taralyn
Taralynn
Taree
Taren
Tari
Tarin
Tarina
Tarja

Tarni
Tarra
Tarrah
Tarren
Tarsam
Tarsha
Tarsila
Taryn
Tarynn
TaŠa
Tasahni
Tasanee
Tasha
Tashanay
Tashina
Tasi
Tasia
Taslima
Tasmine
Tasneem
Tasnim
Tassiana
Tasya
Tate
Tateleigh
Tatem
Tateum
Tatiana
Tatianna
Tatiara
Tatienne
Tatjana
Tattina
Tatum
Tatyana
Tatyanah
Tatyanna
Tauriel
Tausha
Tavi
Tavia
Tavie
Tavor
Tavora
Tawakel
Tawana

Tawanda
Tawanna
Tawnee
Tawney
Tawni
Tawnie
Tawny
Tawnya
Taya
Tayana
Tayci
Tayen
Tayga
Tayla
Taylah
Taylee
Tayler
Tayleur
Taylie
Taylin
Taylor
Taylore
Taylynne
Taynee
Taysia
Taythan
Taytum
Tayvia
Tazashia
Tea
Teagan
Teaghan
Teal
Teale
Teann
Tecla
Teddy
Teegan
Teela
Teena
Tegan
Teghan
Tegwen
Tehani
Tehila
Tehilla

Tehillah
Tehya
Tehzlyn
Teia
Teigan
Teila
Teirra
Teisha
Teja
Tejinder
Tekla
Telina
Tellervo
Telma
Temily
Temperance
Tempest
Tempeste
Tempie
Temple
Temwa
Tena
Tenaya
Tender
Teneca
Tenesha
Tenika
Tenisha
Tenley
Tennessee
Tennie
Tennille
Teodora
Teodozia
Teofila
Tera
Terabithia
Tererai
Teresa
Terese
Teresia
Teresita
Teressa
Tereza
Teri
Terilyn

Terin
Terra
Terralien
Terri
Terrie
Terry
Tertia
Terttu
Teryn
Tesalyn
Tesca
Teshla
Tesia
Tesla
Tesni
Tesoro
Tess
Tessa
Tessaly
Tessara
Tessie
Tethys
Tetyana
Teva
Tevis
Texanna
Texas
Teyanna
Teyarna
Thaddea
Thaia
Thailiagh
Thais
Thaisa
Thalassa
Thalatha
Thaleia
Thalia
Thalie
Thalissa
Thallo
Thamen
Thandeka
Thandi
Thandie
Thandiwe

Thanet
Thao
Thea
Theadora
Thecla
Theda
Theia
Thekla
Thelma
Thembeka
Themis
Theo
Theoda
Theodocia
Theodora
Theodosia
Theofania
Theola
Theone
Theoni
Theophania
Theophanie
Theophila
Theora
Theres
Theresa
Therese
Theresia
Theryn
Thessaly
Theta
Thetis
Thia
Thisbe
Thomasin
Thomasina
Thomasine
Thomasyn
Thomasyne
Thora
Thuy
Thyia
Thyme
Thyone
Thyra
Thyrra

Tia
Tiahna
Tiana
Tianna
Tiara
Tiaret
Tiarna
Tiarne
Tiarra
Ticha
Tiegan
Tiera
Tierney
Tierra
Tiersa
Tierza
Tif
Tifa
Tiffani
Tiffanie
Tiffany
Tiffin
Tiffiney
Tiffiny
Tiffney
Tiffy
Tiger Lily
Tigerlily
Tiggy
Tihana
Tiia
Tiina
Tijana
Tijuana
Tika
Tikal
Tikvah
Tilda
Tilde
Tilder
Tilia
Tilla
Tillie
Tilly
Tilney
Timandra

Timara
Timaree
Timarion
Timberlake
Timberly
Timbre
Timbrel
Timea
Timna
Timothea
Tina
Tinaya
Tinder
Tindra
Tine
Tinka
Tinley
Tinny
Tinsley
Tinuviel
Tiny
Tionne
Tiphany
Tipper
Tirienne
Tiril
Tirion
Tirtza
Tirtzah
Tirzah
Tisa
Tish
Tisha
Tishala
Tishia
Titania
Titina
Tiye
Tiziana
Tobi
Tobin
Toby
Tocara
Toccara
Tohru
Toi

Toiya
Tokka
Tomasa
Tomeka
Tomika
Tomiko
Tomlin
Tommi
Tommiah
Tommie
Tomoko
Tonantzin
Tone
Toni
Tonia
Tonja
Tonje
Tonna
Tonya
Tooba
Tootsie
Topanga
Topaz
Tora
Torah
Torbjørg
Tordis
Torhild
Tori
Torianna
Torie
Toril
Torild
Torill
Torrance
Torre
Torrie
Torunn
Tosca
Toscana
Tosha
Toshiko
Tottie
Toula
Toulane
Tourin

Tova
Tovah
Tove
Towanda
Townley
Toy
Toya
Toyah
Tracee
Tracena
Tracey
Traci
Tracie
Tracina
Tracy
Tram
Tranquility
Trazana
Treasa
Treasure
Treasures
Treemonisha
Treena
Trena
Trenay
Trenna
Tresa
Treslyn
Tressa
Tressie
Tressye
Treva
Trevlin
Treya
Trianna
Tricia
Trijntje
Trilby
Trillian
Trillium
Trina
Trine
Trini
Trinidad
Trinity
Triona

Tripat
Tris
Trish
Trisha
Trissa
Trista
Tristan
Tristana
Tristen
Tristine
Tristyn
Trix
Trixie
Troian
Troya
Tru
Trude
Trudie
Trudy
Truelian
Truely
Trula
Truly
Truvy
Tryphena
Trysta
Tsega
Tsunade
Tsuru
Tucker
Tuesday
Tui
Tula
Tulin
Tulip
Tulisa
Tullia
Tully
Tulsi
Tunde
Tündér
Tundra
Tupelo
Tuppence
Turandot
Turid

Turkessa
Turner
Turquoise
Tushara
Tuuli
Tuva
Tuyet
Tyra

U

Uaine
Ujana
Ulani
Ulrika
Ulrike
Ultima
Ulvhild
Ulyana
Ulyssa
Uma
Umbelina
Umbria
Ume
Umeko
Una
Undie
Undine
Unhei
Unice
Unique
Unita
Unity
Unn
Unni
Urania
Urassaya
Urni

Urraca
Ursa
Ursina
Ursula
Urszula
Urtė
Uruma
Usha
Uzma

V

Vala
  Valancy
  Valarece
  Valarie
  Valborg
  Valda
  Valdine
  Vale
  Valencia
  Valera
  Valeria
  Valerie
  Valerija
  Valeriya
  Valery
  Valeska
  Valetta
  Valia
  Valina
  Valinda
  Valka
  Valkíria
  Valkyrie
  Vallee
  Valleri
  Valli
  Vallie

Vally
Valma
Valmay
Valorie
Valpuri
Valriana
Valya
Valyn
Vancha
Vandana
Vandra
Vanellope
Vanesa
Vanessa
Vanessza
Vanetta
Vangie
Vani
Vanity
Vanja
Vanna
Vannie
Vanora
Varduhi
Varsha
Varsnie
Varvara
Vasantha
Vasanti
Vashanti
Vashti
Vasilia
Vasiliki
Vasilisa
Vasilissa
Vassie
Vaughn
Vauneda
Vavy
Vayden
Vayla
Vaylyn
VeAnn
Veatriki
Vechta
Veda

Veera
Vega
Vela
Velda
Velia
Velina
Vella
Velma
Velta
Velva
Velvet
Vena
Vendetta
Venessa
Venetia
Venezia
Venice
Venita
Venla
Venus
Venya
Veola
Vera
Verda
Verdiana
Verdie
Vered
Verena
Verene
Verenice
Vergie
Verica
Veridian
Verily
Verity
Verla
Verlene
Verlie
Verlyn
Verna
Vernee
Vernell
Vernice
Vernie
Vernita
Verochka

Verolyn
Verona
Verone
Veronica
Veronicah
Veronika
Veroniki
Veronique
Versie
Verta
Vertie
Veruca
Veruschke
Verusha
Verveine
Veryan
Veslemøy
Vesna
Vesper
Vespera
Vesta
Veta
Veva
Vezna
Vhana
Vi
Via
Vianey
Vianna
Vianne
Vianney
Viatrix
Vibeke
Vicenta
Vickey
Vicki
Vickie
Vicky
Victoire
Victoria
Victorine
Victory
Vida
Vidalia
Vidya
Vienna

Vienne
Vierra
Vigdis
Viiu
Viivi
Vika
Vikki
Viktoria
Viktorie
Viktorija
Viktoriya
Vilda
Vilde
Villette
Vilma
Vina
Vincenza
Vincenzina
Vineeta
Vinia
Vinnie
Viola
Violanda
Violante
Violet
Violeta
Violetta
Violette
Viona
Vionnet
Viori
Viorica
Virelai
Virgene
Virgia
Virgie
Virginia
Virginie
Viridiana
Viridis
Virnell
Visitación
Visnja
Vissia
Vita
Vitani

Vitina
Vitória
Vittoria
Viv
Viva
Vivaldi
Viveca
Vivetta
Vivi
Vivia
Vivian
Vivica
Vivien
Vlasta
Voe
Vrai

W

Wafiya
  Waheeda
  Wakana
  Walda
  Waleska
  Walker
  Wallis
  Walterena
  Waltraud
  Wanda
  Waneca
  Wanelle
  Waneta
  Wangari
  Wanita
  Wanjiku
  Wara
  Wava
  Waverley
  Waverly
  Waylin
  Waylyn
  Waynoka
  Wayonka
  Weasy
  Wednesday
  Welles

Welsley
Wenche
Wenda
Wendi
Wendie
Wendla
Wendolyn
Wendy
Wenona
Weronika
Wesleigh
Weslyn
Westly
Westlyn
Whim
Whisper
Whitley
Whitney
Whitter
Whittier
Wietske
Wiktoria
Wilda
Wilder
Wilderness
Wilhelmina
Wilhelmine
Willa
Willamina
Willene
Willia
Willie
Williemae
Willodean
Willona
Willow
Wilma
Wilsonia
Windflower
Windy
Winema
Wineva
Winifred
Winifrid
Winna
Winnette

Winnie
Winnifred
Winola
Winona
Winry
Winslet
Winslow
Winsome
Winter
Winter Breeze
Wiola
Wisteria
Witlee
Wolfie
Wonder
Wren
Wynonna

X

Xandra
Xandy
Xandri
Xandria
Xantara
Xanthe
Xanthea
Xanthia
Xanthis
Xanti
Xara
Xavia
Xavianna
Xaviera
Xavière
Xayla
Xe'Nedra
Xena
Xenia
Xenobia
Xeona
Xhanell
Xhesika
Xhivani
Xhuliana
Xia
Xiamara

Ximena
Xina
Xiomara
Xiomya
Xionara
Xiou
Xochie
Xochitl
Xoe
Xoey
Xosha
Xristina
Xuan
Xylia

Y

Yadira
Yafa
Yaire
Yajaira
Yamilet
Yamileth
Yamilette
Yana
Yancey
Yanel
Yaneli
Yaneliz
Yanelly
Yanely
Yanina
Yanira
Yannah
Yannick
Yanshi
Yara
Yardleigh
Yardley
Yareli
Yarelli
Yarely
Yaretzi
Yarielis

Yaritza
Yashodhara
Yasi
Yasmeen
Yasmin
Yasmina
Yasmine
Yasoda
Yassa
Yassamin
Yaumara
Yaya
Yayla
Yazia
Yazmin
Yazmyne
Yeardley
Yehudis
Yehudit
Yekaterina
Yekira
Yelena
Yelka
Yemanji
Yemen
Yemima
Yennifer
Yera
Yesenia
Yesica
Yessenia
Yessica
Yetta
Yeva
Yevdokiya
Yevette
Yevgeniya
Yezenia
Ygritte
Yianna
Yiasemi
Yildiz
Yiona
Ylenia
Ylva
Yma

Ynez
Yngvild
Yoanna
Yobhel
Yocheved
Yoela
Yohanna
Yoki
Yoko
Yoksan
Yolanda
Yolande
Yolany
Yolonda
Yonina
Yonit
Yoobin
Yoselin
Yoshiko
Youna
Yriana
Yrsa
Ysabeau
Ysabel
Ysabella
Ysaline
Ysanne
Ysbal
Ysela
Ysella
Yselle
Yseult
Ysobelle
Ysolde
Yue
Yui
Yuki
Yukia
Yukiko
Yuko
Yuliana
Yulianna
Yulissa
Yuliya
Yume
Yumi

Yumna
Yuna
Yunoka
Yunuen
Yuridia
Yurika
Yusra
Yustina
Yuvia
Yuzu

Z

Zabby
Zabrina
Zada
Zadie
Zady
Zaelia
Zafira
Zafrina
Zafyra
Zaha
Zahara
Zahava
Zaheera
Zahli
Zahlia
Zahra
Zaia
Zaida
Zaide
Zaidee
Zaile
Zailey
Zaily
Zaina
Zainab
Zaira
Zakelina

Zakeya
Zakira
Zakiya
Zakiyah
Żaklina
Zakya
Zali
Zalika
Zalira
Zaltana
Zalyn
Zamia
Zamora
Zana
Zandra
Zandy
Zane
Zaneeta
Zaneta
Zaniah
Zanita
Zaniyah
Zanna
Zanta
Zanthe
Zanya
Zaor
Zapressa
Zara
Zarah
Zareah
Zareen
Zari
Zaria
Zariah
Zarie
Zarifa
Zarina
Zarita
Zariyah
Zarya
Zatanna
Zaya
Zayda
Zayla
Zaylee

Zaylia
Zaylie
Zaylynn Rain
Zayn
Zayna
Zaynab
Zayra
Zayva
Zaza
Zazie
Zdislava
Zee
Zeely
Zeenat
Zefira
Zeina
Zeisha
Zeituni
Zel
Zela
Zelah
Zelda
Zelena
Zelia
Zelie
Zelinda
Zeline
Zella
Zelma
Zelpha
Zemarah
Zemirah
Zena
Zenaida
Zenaide
Zenda
Zendaya
Zenia
Zenida
Zenisha
Zenith
Zenna
Zenobia
Zenolia
Zenovia
Zephie

Zephyr
Zephyrine
Zepour
Zera
Zerelda
Zeriah
Zerlina
Zerna
Zeta
Zethra
Zetta
Zettie
Zevvi
Zeya
Zeynep
Zhaklina
Zhanet
Zhanna
Zhenya
Zhinni
Zia
Ziana
Zielissa
Zilee
Zilia
Zilla
Zillah
Zillana
Zilpha
Zilphia
Zilynn
Zina
Zinaida
Zinnia
Zinovia
Zinoviya
Zion
Zipporah
Zira
Zissy
Zita
Ziva
Ziyi
Zlata
Zoa
Zobia

Zoda
Zoe
Zoelie
Zoeline
Zoella
Zoelle
Zoey
Zoeya
Zofia
Zoha
Zohal
Zoi
Zoie
Zoila
Zola
Zona
Zonnie
Zooey
Zophia
Zora
Zoraida
Zoraïde
Zoraya
Zoriana
Zorica
Zorka
Zosia
Zosima
Zowie
Zoya
Zulema
Zureen

PART II

BOYS NAMES

A

Aaden
Aadem
Aadne
Aadolf
Aahrok
Aahron
Aali
Aalim
Aaradhya
Aarian
Aariyeh
Aaro
Aaron
Aart
Aaru
Aatu
Aayden
Aban
Abanoub
Abasi
Abaven
Abayomi
Abbin
Abbott
Abdallah
Abdiel
Abdul

Abdullah
Abdulrahman
Abe
Abed
Abel
Abelard
Abelardo
Aberforth
Abey
Abhay
Abhaya
Abhi
Abhijeet
Abhinav
Abhishek
Abiah
Abie
Abiel
Abimael
Abimanyu
Abner
Abraham
Abrahama
Abrahamu
Abrahin
Abrahim
Abrahm
Abrahon
Abrakham
Abram
Abramo
Abran
Abraram
Abrax
Abraxas
Abriel
Absalom
Absalon
Absolom
Abuchi
Acacio
Ace
Acelin
Achebe
Acheron
Achille

Achilles
Achilleus
Achim
Acie
Ackerley
Ackley
Actaeon
Acton
Adahy
Adair
Adalberto
Adalwolf
Adam
Adamo
Adan
adar
Adare
Addison
Ade
Adelard
Adelbert
Adelmo
Aden
Adek
Adern
Adert
Adiel
Adil
Adim
Adin
Adisa
Adison
Aditya
Adlai
Adler
Adley
Admir
Admiral
Admon
Adnan
Adolf
Adolfo
Adolph
Adolphus
Adonai
Adone

Adoniah
Adoniram
Adonis
Adriaan
Adrian
Adriano
Adrianus
Adric
Adriel
Adrien
Adrik
Adryan
Adventure
Aedan
Aegidius
Aegir
Aelius
Aemon
Aeneas
Aengus
Aenon
Aenor
Aeric
Aerlin
Aerol
Aeryn
Aeson
Aesten
Aetius
Aevryn
Afonso
Agamemnon
Agamjot
Agan
Agapito
Agathon
Agimar
Agin
Aginhart
Agnello
Agnus
Agostino
Agurys
Agustin
Ahab
Aharon

Ahijah
Ahmad
Ahmed
Aidah
Aidan
Aiden
Aidenn
Aidric
Aidyn
Aiken
Ailben
Ailik
Ailil
Ailm
Aimen
Aimery
Aindreas
Aindriu
Ainsley
Airyck
Aithan
Aitor
Ajahni
Ajani
Ajax
Ajay
Ajinder
Ajit
Akash
Åke
Akeem
Akiba
Akili
Akim
Akio
Akira
Akito
Akiva
Aklen
Akon
Akor
Aksel
Akseli
Akshat
Akshay
Al

Ala
Aladdin
Alai
Alain
Alan
Alaric
Alasdair
Alastair
Alastar
Alastor
Alazander
Alazar
Alban
Albe
Albee
Alben
Alberic
Albert
Alberto
Albertos
Albertus
Albie
Albin
Albino
Albion
Albrecht
Albright
Albus
Alby
Alcaeus
Alcander
Alcee
Alcide
Alcuin
Alden
Alder
Aldis
Aldo
Aldous
Aldric
Aldrich
Aldrin
Aldus
Aldwyn
Alec
Aleczander

Aleem
Alef
Aleister
Aleix
Alejandro
Alejo
Alek
Alekos
Aleksan
Aleksandar
Aleksander
Aleksanteri
Aleksei
Aleksi
Aleph
Aleron
Alessandro
Alessio
Alex
Alexander
Alexandre
Alexandreus
Alexandro
Alexandros
Alexandru
Alexavier
Alexei
Alexi
Alexian
Alexios
Alexis
Alexzander
Alf
Alif
Alfie
Alfons
Alfonso
Alfonzo
Alford
Alfred
Alfredo
Algene
Alger
Algernon
Algie
Ali

Alim
Alijah
Alik
Alikanderix
Alim
Alistair
Alister
Alixander
Allan
Allegro
Allen
Allie
Allison
Allouette
Allyn
Alma
Almanzo
Almond
Almus
Alner
Alois
Aloise
Aloisio
Alojz
Alok
Alon
Alonso
Alonza
Alonzo
Aloys
Aloysius
Alper
Alpertti
Alpha
Alphaeus
Alphard
Alpheus
Alphonse
Alphonser
Alpih
Alpin
Alric
Altair
Altan
Alter
Alto

Alton
Alucard
Alun
Alva
Alvah
Alvan
Alvar
Alvaro
Alvary
Alveera
Alvie
Alvin
Alvis
Alvy
Alwin
Alyl
Alyn
Alyosha
Amachi
Amadeo
Amadeus
Amadi
Amado
Amador
Amadou
Amadour
Amahl
Amalric
Aman
Amani
Amar
Amare
Amari
Amarion
Amaro
Amaru
Amasa
Amaury
Ambrogio
Ambroise
Ambroos
Ambrose
Ambrosio
Ambrosio
Ambrosius
Amco

Amedep
Ameer
Americo
Americus
Amel
Amery
Ames
Amias
Amiel
Amik
Amintore
Amir
Amiri
Amit
Amitabh
Amitai
Ammar
Ammon
Amnon
Amon
Amondo
Amor
Amory
Amos
Amran
Amram
Amrik
Amyas
Amycus
Anacleto
Anacletus
Anakin
Ananias
Anaru
Anastacio
Anastasios
Anastasius
Anat
Anatole
Anatoly
Anaxander
Ancel
Anchor
Anchorage
Ander
Anders

Anderson
Andersonn
Andin
Andon
Andor
Andra
Andrak
Andranik
Andre
Andrea
Andreas
Andrees
Andrei
Andrej
Andrejs
Andreo
Andres
Andreu
Andreus
Andrew
Andrey
Andrezj
Andric
Andries
Andrii
Andrija
Andrin
Andris
Andrius
Andriy
Androcles
Andros
Andrus
Andrzej
Andy
Aneeque
Anes
Aneil
Aneurin
Angel
Angelo
Angelos
Angie
Angus
Anibal
Aniceto

Anik
Aniket
Anil
Animal
Anis
Anker
Anndra
Annibale
Anns
Annunziato
Ansel
Anselm
Anselmo
Ansem
Ansgar
Anshul
Ansillo
Anson
Antero
Anthem
Anthony
Antidote
Antioch
Antione
Antoine
Anton
Antone
Antonello
Antoni
Antonin
Antonino
Antonio
Antonios
Antonius
Antony
Antti
Antwan
Antwon
Anwar
Anxo
Aodh
Aodhan
Apolinar
Apollo
Apollon
Apostolos

Apu
Aqil
Aquarius
Ara
Arabian
Aragon
Aragorn
Aram
Aramis
Arandu
Arash
Arashi
Aravind
Araz
Arcadio
Arcangelo
Arch
Archer
Archibald
Archie
Archil
Archimedes
Archon
Arcturus
Arda
Ardell
Arden
Ardghal
Ardian
Ardo
Are
Arel
Ares
Argaeus
Argent
Argon
Argos
Argus
Arop
Ari
Ariah
Arian
Arias
Aric
Arie
Arieh

Ariel
Arier
Aries
Arik
Arild
Aris
Ariss
Aristeo
Aristide
Aristides
Ariston
Aristotle
Arius
Arjen
Arjun
Arkadios
Arkadiusz
Arkadiy
Arkady
Arki
Arlan
Arland
Arlen
Arley
Arlie
Arlin
Arling
Arlington
Arlis
Arliss
Arlo
Arlow
Armaan
Arman
Armand
Armando
Armani
Armeet
Armel
Armen
Armikka
Armin
Armistead
Armond
Armstrong
Arnaldo

Arnau
Arnaud
Arnav
Arne
Arnie
Arnish
Arno
Arnold
Arnoldo
Arnulfo
Aroldo
Aron
Arrak
Arram
Arran
Arrigo
Arrington
Arron
Arrow
Arsen
Arsep
Arsenio
Arsenios
Arseniusz
Arseniy
Arshaluys
Art
Artair
Artem
Artemas
Artemio
Artemis
Artemus
Arther
Arthur
Artie
Artin
Artis
Artoun
Arttu
Artturi
Artur
Arturo
Artyom
Arun
Arunabh

Arvel
Arvid
Arvil
Arvin
Arvind
Arvo
Arwen
Arwyn
Ary
Aryan
Aryeh
Asa
Asad
Asael
Asafa
Asaiah
Asani
Asante
Asan
Asaph
Ascencion
Ascher
Aschton
Asdrubal
Ash
Asha
Ashal
Ashby
Asher
Ashley
Ashok
Ashraf
Ashton
Ashwin
Ashworth
Asier
Asif
Aslan
Aspen
Asriel
Aster
Astin
Aston
Astor
Astrophel
Asuncion

Ataman
Atanas
Athan
Athanasios
Athanasius
Athelstan
Athen
Athol
Athos
Atilla
Atlas
Atlee
Atom
Aton
Atreides
Atreyu
Atrius
Atrus
Atrush
Atticai
Atticus
Attila
Attilio
Attison
Atul
Atz
Auberon
Aubrey
Auden
Audie
Audrey
Audun
Augie
August
Augustan
Augustas
Auguste
Augusten
Augustijn
Augustin
Augustine
Augusto
Augustus
Aulay
Aurèle
Aurelian

Aurelien
Aurelio
Aurelius
Auren
Auric
Austell
Austen
Auster
Austeyn
Austin
Auston
Austyn
Auther
Author
Avan
Averett
Averil
Averill
Avery
Avett
Avgoustinos
Avi
Avie
Avien
Avier
Avin
Avitus
Aviv
Avneet
Avon
Avory
Avram
Avraam
Avram
Avriah
Avrian
Avrohom
Avrum
Avtar
Awnan
Awsten
Axel
Axl
Axton
Ayaan
Ayal

Ayaz
Aydan
Ayden
Aydin
Ayers
Ayler
Ayman
Aymeric
Ayo
Ayron
Ayrton
Ayub
Ayvin
Azarel
Azariah
Azaryah
Aziz
Azizul
Azizun
Azizus

B

Babah
  Baban
  Babar
  Baby
  Baden
  Badi
  Badil
  Baer
  Bagheera
  Bahal
  Bahran
  Bailey
  Bailos
  Baird
  Baken
  Baker
  Balanchine
  Balbeem
  Balbeer
  Baldassare
  Baldev
  Baldovino
  Baldur
  Baldwin
  Balen
  Balian
  Balin

Balis
Ballard
Balminder
Baltazar
Balthazar
Balvinder
Bando
Bandos
Bane
Banister
Banjo
Banks
Banner
Bannon
Banquo
Baptiste
Barack
Barak
Baraka
Barbara
Barclay
Bard
Bardot
Barend
Baris
Barker
Barke
Barna
Barnabah
Barnabas
Barnaby
Barnard
Barnes
Barney
Baron
Barrett
Barrie
Barrik
Barrington
Barun
Barry
Bart
Bartek
Bartemius
Bartholomeus
Bartlomiej

Barto
Bartok
Bartolomeo
Bartolomeu
Barton
Bartosz
Barty
Baruch
Barwon
Bas
Bascom
Bash
Bashir
Basil
Basilio
Basim
Basse
Bastian
Bastien
Batu
Baudelaire
Baudouin
Bauer
Bautista
Baxley
Baxter
Bayar
Bayard
Bayes
Baylen
Baylin
Baylor
Bayne
Baynes
Bayo
Baz
Bazah
Bazil
Beale
Bear
Beau
Beaudan
Beauden
Beaumont
Beauregard
Beaux

Beauxregard
Beck
Becker
Beckett
Beckham
Bede
Bedford
Bedrot
Bee
Beecher
Behrouz
Bejit
Bela
Belarius
Bellamy
Belvin
Ben
Benaiah
Benar
Bence
Benedek
Benedet
Benedict
Benedito
Benen
Beniah
Beniamino
Benicio
Benigno
Benito
Benjamen
Benjamim
Benjamin
Benjen
Benji
Bennet
Bennett
Bennie
Bennison
Benno
Benny
Benok
Benoni
Bensen
Bent
Benson

Bentlee
Bentley
Bently
Benton
Bentar
Benyamin
Benzion
Beorn
Beppe
Beppet
Berdon
Bereket
Beren
Berenger
Beres
Berge
Bergen
Beriah
Beric
Berj
Berjik
Berkeley
Berkley
Berlin
Bernard
Bernardo
Bernett
Bernhard
Bernie
Bernon
Bernt
Berry
Bert
Bertalan
Berthold
Bertholdt
Berthony
Bertie
Berto
Berton
Bertur
Bertrand
Berwyn
Beryl
Besnik
Beto

Bettino
Betzalel
Bevan
Beverly
Bhajan
Bhavan
Bhavin
Biagio
Biel
Bienvenido
Bilal
Bilbo
Bill
Billie
Billy
Bing
Binghan
Biniyam
Binyamin
Bion
Birch
Birchard
Birger
Birhanu
Birk
Bishop
Bix
Bixby
Bjarne
Bjarni
Bjorn
Blas
Blade
Bladen
Blaine
Blair
Blaise
Blake
Blanc
Blane
Blanket
Blas
Blase
Blaynen
Blayson
Blayz

Blayze
Blazen
Blazej
Blazhe
Bleiz
Bligh
Blinn
Blitz
Blixa
Bloom
Blue
Blues
Boam
Boa
Boaz
Bob
Bobak
Bobbie
Bobby
BoDamian
Bode
Bodee
Boden
Bodhi
Bodie
Bogdan
Boghos
Bogumil
Bohdan
Bojan
Bolesław
Bolt
Bomani
Bonaventura
Bonaventure
Bond
Boniface
Bonifacio
Bonifaz
Booker
Boomer
Boone
Booth
Boq
Bora
Boril

Boris
Boromir
Borys
Bosco
Boston
Boswell
Botond
Bowden
Bowdoin
Bowen
Bowie
Bowman
Bowyer
Boyce
Boycek
Boyd
Bozeman
Braam
Brace
Bracken
Brad
Bradan
Braddock
Braddon
Braden
Bradford
Bradie
Bradley
Bradly
Bradon
Brady
Bradyn
Braeden
Braedin
Braedon
Braedyn
Braelin
Bragi
Brahms
Braiden
Braison
Braith
Bram
Bramwell
Bran
Branan

Brancen
Branch
Brand
Brandan
Branden
Brander
Brando
Brandon
Brandt
Brandy
Brandyn
Brannen
Brannigan
Brannock
Brannon
Branson
Brant
Brantlee
Brantley
Branwell
Brasen
Braston
Braulio
Braun
Bravery
Braxson
Braxton
Bray
Brayan
Braychan
Braydan
Brayden
Braydon
Braylen
Brayley
Braylon
Brayson
Brayton
Brazen
Breaker
Breccan
Breck
Breckan
Brecken
Brecki
Brekkin

Bren
Brendan
Brenden
Brendin
Brendon
Brendus
Brennan
Brennen
Brenner
Brennon
Brennus
Brenon
Brent
Brentley
Brenton
Brentyn
Breock
Brek
Bret
Brett
Brettley
Bretton
Brevin
Brevyn
Brewer
Brewster
Brexton
Breyer
Breyson
Briah
Brian
Brice
Bricen
Brick
Bridger
Bridh
Briek
Brien
Brier
Brigg
Briggs
Brigham
Brighton
Briley
Brindley
Brinton

Brinxton
Brioc
Brion
Brisan
Briscoe
Brishan
Brison
Brisyn
Brit
Briton
Britt
Britton
Brixton
Broadus
Broc
Brock
Brockton
Brodee
Broden
Brodim
Broderick
Brodie
Brody
Brogan
Brokos
Brolin
Broly
Brom
Bromde
Bronc
Bronislaw
Bronson
Bronwyn
Bronx
Bronze
Brook
Brooker
Brooklyn
Brooks
Brown
Browning
Bruce
Bruin
Brunsol
Brunson
Bryan

Bryant
Bryar
Bryce
Brycen
Brychan
Bryden
Brydon
Bryer
Brym
Bryn
Brynner
Bryon
Bryom
Bryshon
Bryson
Bubba
Buchanan
Buck
Buckley
Budil
Buddie
Buddy
Buford
Bukhosi
Burak
Burgess
Burhan
Burke
Burl
Burleigh
Burley
Burn
Burnell
Burney
Burrell
Burt
Burton
Busir
Buster
Buzz
Buzin

C

Cab
    Cabe
    Cable
    Cabot
    Cace
    Cadao
    Cade
    Cadel
    Cadell
    Caden
    Caelan
    Cador
    Cadfael
    Cadmiah
    Cadmon
    Cadmus
    Cadogan
    Cador
    Cadwalader
    Cadwaladr
    Cadwallader
    Caedmon
    Caedyn
    Cael
    Caelan
    Caeleb
    Caelen

Cailean
Caelius
Caellum
Caelum
Caelus
Caetano
Cage
Cagney
Cai
Cain
Caiden
Cail
Cailean
Caillou
Cain
Cainan
Caine
Cainon
Caio
Cairbre
Cairo
Cairon
Caius
Cal
Calais
Calbert
Calcifer
Calder
Caldwell
Cale
Caleb
Caledon
Calem
Calen
Calian
Calil
Calimero
Calin
Calip
Caliph
Calix
Calixte
Calixto
Calixton
Callahan
Callan

Callaway
Callen
Calleo
Callisto
Callum
Calogero
Calum
Calvary
Calvert
Calvin
Calvim
Camdin
Camden
Camdyn
Cameron
Camillo
Camilo
Campbell
Camper
Camren
Camrin
Camron
Camryn
Canan
Candelario
Candido
Candon
Candor
Cane
Cannon
Canon
Cantun
Canute
Canuto
Canyon
Caomh
Capistran
Capper
Cappy
Captain
Caractacus
Caradoc
Caradog
Carantoc
Carbry
Carden

Cardiff
Carey
Carlib
Carlin
Carleton
Carlisle
Carlito
Carlitos
Carlo
Carlos
Carlson
Carlton
Carlyle
Carmelo
Carmen
Carmichael
Carmine
Carnell
Carney
Carol
Carolus
Carper
Carrick
Carrington
Carrizoa
Carro
Carroll
Carrow
Carsen
Carsin
Carsten
Carston
Carter
Carvay
Carver
Carwyn
Cary
Cas
Casanova
Case
Casen
Casey
Cash
Cashel
Cashmere
Cashton

Casimer
Casimir
Casimiro
Cason
Caspar
Casper
Caspian
Cass
Cassander
Cassel
Cassian
Cassidy
Cassiel
Cassini
Cassio
Cassius
Casson
Castiel
Castillon
Castle
Castor
Caswyn
Catalin
Catarino
Cathal
Cathan
Cato
Catullus
Caullin
Cavan
Cavell
Cavin
Cayden
Caydnn
Caydran
Caydren
Cayetano
Caylan
Cayson
Caz
Cecil
Cecilio
Cedar
Cedric
Cedrick
Ceeley

Ceili
Ceiriog
Ceiro
Cejay
Celeste
Celestino
Celio
Celt
Cenobio
Cenweard
Cephas
Cephus
Cereal
Cesar
Cesare
Cetin
Ceyhun
Cezanne
Cezar
Chace
Chad
Chadd
Chadrick
Chadwick
Chael
Chago
Chaim
Chain
Chakaia
Chamkaur
Champion
Chance
Chancellor
Chancelor
Chancy
Chandler
Channer
Channing
Chano
Chanse
Chantzelor
Chap
Chapin
Chaplin
Charanjiv
Chariton

Charl
Charles
Charleston
Charley
Charlie
Charlot
Charlton
Charming
Charon
Chase
Chasen
Chaska
Chaske
Chastin
Chatham
Chaucer
Chauncey
Chava
Chay
Chayo
Chayse
Chaysin
Chaytan
Chayton
Chaz
Chazz
Che
Checo
Chellis
Chelone
Chema
Chencho
Chente
Chepi
Chepo
Cherokee
Chesley
Chesney
Chester
Chet
Chevalier
Chevy
Cheyne
Chicane
Chico
Chilton

Chima
Chip
Chiron
Chivan
Chiwetel
Chord
Chris
Christer
Christiaan
Christian
Christof
Christoffer
Christoph
Christophe
Christopher
Christos
Christyan
Chrysolite
Chubs
Chuck
Chucky
Churchill
Chuuya
Chuy
Ciabhan
Cian
Ciaran
Cicero
Cid
Ciel
Cilix
Cillian
Cimarron
Cinna
Ciprian
Cipriano
Ciriaco
Cirilo
Ciro
Cirocco
Cirroc
Claes
Claiborne
Clair
Claire
Clancy

Clarance
Clare
Claren
Clarence
Clarion
Clark
Clarke
Claud
Claude
Claudie
Claudio
Claudiu
Claudius
Claudy
Claus
Clay
Clayson
Clayten
Clayton
Cleavey
Clell
Clellan
Clem
Clemens
Clement
Clemente
Clemeth
Cleo
Cleofas
Cleon
Cleophas
Clete
Cleto
Cletus
Cleve
Cleveland
Cliff
Clifford
Clifton
Clint
Clinton
Clive
Clovis
Cloyd
Clunie
Clyce

Clyde
Coalfield
Coastal
Cobalt
Cobar
Cobb
Cobee
Coburn
Coby
Coda
Codey
Codie
Codrut
Cody
Coen
Cohen
Coke
Colben
Colbert
Colby
Colden
Cole
Coleman
Coleridge
Coleton
Coley
Colie
Colin
Collier
Collin
Collins
Collison
Colm
Colman
Colorado
Colsen
Colson
Colt
Colten
Colter
Coltin
Colton
Coltrane
Columba
Columbus
Colville

Colwyn
Colyer
Commodore
Conal
Conall
Conan
Conchobar
Coney
Conifer
Conlan
Conley
Connar
Connell
Conner
Connie
Connolly
Connor
Conor
Conrad
Conrado
Conran
Conroy
Constant
Constantijn
Constantin
Constantine
Constantino
Constantinos
Constanzo
Consus
Conway
Coolidge
Cooper
Copernicus
Copland
Copper
Coppola
Corax
Corban
Corbett
Corbin
Corbinian
Corbrae
Corby
Corbyn
Cordell

Corder
Cordovan
Corentin
Corey
Corgan
Coridon
Corin
Corliss
Cormac
Cormack
Cormoran
Corné
Cornelio
Cornelious
Cornelis
Cornelius
Cornell
Corradino
Corrado
Corrin
Corrion
Corsin
Cort
Cortez
Cortland
Cortney
Corvin
Corvus
Corwin
Cory
Corzen
Cosimo
Cosmas
Cosme
Cosmin
Cosmo
Cosmos
Costantino
Costel
Coster
Costin
Cotter
Cotton
Coty
Coulson
Coulter

Courage
Court
Courtland
Courtney
Cove
Covin
Covington
Cowan
Cowen
Coy
Coyote
Crad
Craig
Crandall
Crane
Crash
Crawford
Cray
Crayton
Creasy
Creed
Creedence
Creighton
Crescencio
Crescenzo
Cresson
Creston
Crew
Crews
Crighton
Crimson
Cris
Crisanto
Crispin
Crispino
Crispus
Cristian
Cristiano
Cristobal
Cristofer
Cristoforo
Cristopher
Crockett
Crofton
Croix
Cromwell

Cronan
Crosby
Cross
Crosson
Crowley
Crue
Cruiz
Crusoe
Cruz
Csaba
Cuan
Cuauhtemoc
Cubby
Cuco
Cuin
Cuitlahuac
Cullen
Cullin
Cupid
Curley
Curran
Currer
Currie
Currier
Curt
Curtis
Curtiss
Cuthbert
Cutler
Cutter
Cuyle
Cy
Cyan
Cylar
Cyler
Cymbeline
Cynan
Cynric
Cypher
Cypress
Cyprian
Cyprus
Cyriac
Cyril
Cyrille
Cyrus

D

Daan
  Dabney
  Dacian
  Dade
  Daegan
  Daelan
  Daevon
  Dafydd
  Dag
  Dagan
  Dager
  Dagon
  Dagwood
  Dahy
  Daichi
  Daimon
  Dain
  Dainen
  Daip
  Daisley
  Daisuke
  Dakar
  Dakari
  Damari
  Dakoda
  Dakota
  Dakotah

Dalan
Dale
Dalee
Dalen
Daley
Daljit
Dallan
Dallas
Dallen
Dallin
Dallon
Dally
Dalton
Daly
Damek
Dalyn
Damani
Damarcus
Damari
Damarion
Dameon
Damian
Damiano
Damien
Damion
Damir
Dammes
Damocles
Damon
Dan
Dana
Danail
Danar
Dandre
Dane
Daneel
Danell
Dangelo
Danger
Danial
Danian
Daniel
Daniele
Danielius
Daniil
Danijel

Danilo
Daniyal
Danner
Dannie
Dannin
Danny
Dante
Danuel
Danyal
Danyl
Danzig
Daoud
Daquan
Dara
Darby
Darcus
Darcy
Dardan
Dare
Darek
Darell
Daren
Dari
Darian
Dariel
Darien
Darin
Dario
Darion
Darius
Darko
Darl
Darnell
Darold
Daron
Darragh
Darrel
Darrell
Darren
Darrian
Darrick
Darrien
Darrin
Darrion
Darrium
Darrius

Darron
Darrow
Darryl
Darshan
Dartagnan
Darvin
Darwin
Daryl
Daryle
Daryus
Dash
Dashawn
Dashel
Dashiell
Dastan
Daud
Daughtry
Daunte
Davante
Dave
Daven
Daveth
Davey
Davi
Davian
David
Davide
Davin
Davinder
Davion
Davis
Davison
Davit
Davon
Davonte
Davor
Davy
Davyd
Dawid
Dawit
Dawood
Dawson
Dawud
Dax
Daxon
Daxton

Daxx
Dayal
Dayl
Dayle
Daylen
Daylon
Daymion
Daymon
Daynan
Dayton
Deacon
Deagan
Dean
Deandre
Deane
Deangelo
Decarus
Decatur
Decker
Declan
DeCota
Dedric
Dedrick
Dee
Deegan
Deepak
Deepan
Deion
Deison
Deja
Dejan
Dejuan
Deke
Dekker
Deklan
Del
Delan
Delancy
Delane
Delano
Delbert
Dell
Delmar
Delmas
Delmer
Delos

Delson
Delton
Delvan
Delvin
Demarco
Demarcus
Demario
Demarion
Demas
Demetre
Demetri
Demetrio
Demetrios
Demetris
Demetrius
Demian
Demitri
Demond
Demonte
Dempsey
Demyan
Denahi
Denali
Denard
Denah
Denham
Denholm
Denim
Denis
Deniz
Dennie
Dennis
Dennison
Denny
Deno
Denton
Denver
Denys
Denzel
Denzil
Denzin
Deon
Deondre
Deondrey
Deonta
Deontae

Deontay
Deonte
Deontez
Dequan
Dereck
Derek
Derenzo
Dereon
Derian
Deric
Derice
Derick
Derik
Dermot
Deron
Derrek
Derrell
Derrick
Derrin
Derry
Derwin
Derwyn
Deshaun
Deshawn
Deshon
Desiderio
Desman
Desmond
Destery
Destiel
Destin
Destrier
Destry
Detlef
Detlev
Detton
Deuce
Dev
Devak
Deval
Devan
Devante
Devaris
Deven
Devereaux
Devershi

Devi
Devin
Devlin
Devon
Devonta
Devontae
Devonte
Devyn
Dewayne
Dewey
Dewitt
Dex
Dexter
Dezmond
Dezső
Dhane
Dhani
Dharjath
Dharmvir
Dhiraj
Dhiren
Dhruv
Diablo
Diamantino
Diamond
Diarmad
Diarmid
Diarmuid
Dick
Dickie
Dickinson
Dickon
Dickron
Didier
Didrik
Diederick
Diederik
Diego
Diello
Dierks
Diesel
Dieter
Dietrich
Dietz
Digby
Diggory

Digory
Dikran
Dilan
Dilbert
Dilip
Dillan
Dillard
Dillinger
Dillion
Dillon
Dima
Dimas
Dimitr
Dimitri
Dimitrios
Dimitris
Dimitry
Dimos
Dinesh
Dinis
Dino
Diogenes
Diogo
Diokles
Dion
Dionicio
Dionisio
Dionte
Dior
Dirk
Disung
Divakar
Dixon
Django
Djimon
Dmitri
Dmitriy
Dmitry
Dmytro
Doak
Dobbin
Dobromir
Doc
Dock
Dodge
Dolan

Dolores
Dolph
Dolphus
Dolvett
Domenic
Domenick
Domenico
Domhnall
Domingo
Dominic
Dominick
Dominik
Dominique
Dominykas
Domitilo
Domonkos
Don
Donagh
Donal
Donald
Donaldo
Donat
Donatello
Donatien
Donato
Donavan
Donavon
Donell
Donley
Donn
Donnan
Donncha
Donnell
Donnie
Donny
Donovan
Donovon
Donta
Dontae
Dontay
Donte
Doodlebop
Doolin
Doon
Doran
Dorian

Doric
Dorin
Doron
Dorsey
Dorwin
Doug
Dougal
Dougie
Douglas
Douglass
Dougray
Dov
Dovydas
Dow
Doyle
Dracen
Drachen
Draco
Draden
Dragan
Drago
Dragomir
Dragon
Dragos
Dragoslav
Draisen
Drake
Draken
Drakon
Draper
Draven
Draycen
Drayden
Drayke
Drayson
Drayton
Drazik
Dreamer
Dreden
Dresden
Drew
Drexel
Dryden
Drystan
Du Toit
Duane

Duard
Duarte
Dublin
Dudley
Duff
Dugan
Duke
Dulé
Dumbledore
Dumer
Dumisani
Dumitru
Duncan
Dunstan
Durante
Durham
Durward
Durwood
Dušan
Dustin
Dusty
Dutch
Dutton
Duwayne
Dwain
Dwaine
Dwane
Dwayne
Dwight
Dwyer
Dyami
Dylan
Dyson

E

Eames
Eamon
Ean
Earendel
Earl
Earle
Earlie
Earvin
Early
Earnest
Eason
Eastman
Easton
Eathan
Eato
Ebb
Eben
Ebenezer
Eberardo
Ebert
Ebrahim
Ed
Edd
Eddie
Eddison
Eddy
Edel

Eden
Edern
Edgar
Edgardo
Edge
Edgerton
Edin
Edison
Edmar
Edme
Edmond
Edmund
Edmundo
Edo
Edoardo
Edric
Edsel
Edson
Eduard
Eduardo
Edur
Edvard
Edvin
Edward
Edwardo
Edwin
Eeli
Eelis
Eemeli
Eemil
Eero
Eetu
Efraim
Efrain
Efren
Efstathios
Egan
Egidio
Egil
Egon
Egypt
Ehlii
Ehren
Ehsan
Ehud
Eian

Eiel
Eiger
Eilam
Eilif
Eillic
Eimhin
Einar
Eino
Eion
Eirik
Eirwyn
Eissa
Eitan
Eivind
Eizzyk
Elad
Eladio
Elam
Elan
Elbert
Elbhen

Eldar
Elden
Elder
Eldon
Eldra
Eldred
Eldridge
Eleazar
Elgan
Elgar
Elgin
Elhanan
Eli
Elia
Eliah
Eliam
Elian
Elias
Eliaz
Eliel
Eliet
Eliezer
Elige
Eligius

Elihu
Elijah
Elio
Eliodoro
Elior
Eliot
Eliott
Elis
Eliseo
Eliseu
Elisha
Eliu
Eliyahu
Eljas
Elkan
Ellar
Ellery
Ellick
Elling
Ellington
Elliot
Elliott
Ellis
Ellison
Ellsworth
Ellwood
Elmer
Elmo
Elmore
Eloi
Elop
Eloy
Elpidio
Elric
Elroy
Elson
Elton
Elvan
Elvin
Elvis
Elwin
Elwood
Elwyn
Elwynn
Ely
Elyas

Elysian
Elza
Elzie
Emad
Emanuel
Emanuele
Ember
Emeka
Emerett
Emeric
Emerick
Emeril
Emerson
Emery
Emeryk
Emet
Emeterio
Emidio
Emiel
Emigdio
Emil
Emile
Emilian
Emiliano
Emilio
Emir
Emlyn
Emmanouil
Emmanuel
Emmerich
Emmet
Emmeton
Emmett
Emmin
Emmitt
Emory
Emre
Emric
Emry
Emrys
Emyr
Enapay
Enda
Ender
Endre
Endrit

Endymion
Enea
Enedin
Enej
Engelbert
Engelberto
Enio
Enjolras
Ennis
Enoch
Enos
Enric
Enrico
Enrique
Ensley
Entriken
Enver
Enzor
Eoghan
Eoin
Eolann
Eomer
Eonan
Ephesian
Ephraim
Ephram
Ephrem
Ephron
Epic
Epifanio
Eppa
Eragon
Erasmo
Erasmus
Erastus
Ercole
Eren
Ergin
Erhard
Erian
Eric
Erian
Erich
Erick
Erickson
Ericson

Erik
Erikson
Erin
Erion
Erkki
Erland
Erlend
Erling
Ermine
Erminio
Ernest
Ernesto
Ernie
Ernst
Eron
Eros
Errol
Erskine
Ervin
Erwin
Eryk
Erysichthon
Eryx
Esai
Esau
Esben
Esca
Escher
Esco
Eskil
Esli
Esmond
Espen
Espiridion
Essex
Essio
Estanislao
Esteban
Estel
Esten
Estephen
Estes
Estevan
Estlin
Ethan
Ethanael

Ethaniel
Ethann
Ethen
Etienne
Ettore
Euan
Eubank
Euclid
Eudes
Euell
Eugene
Eugenio
Eugeniusz
Eulalio
Eusebio
Eustace
Eustache
Eustachio
Eustaquio
Eustolio
Evan
Evanam
Evander
Evandro
Evangel
Evangelos
Evans
Evaristo
Evelyn
Everard
Everardo
Everd
Everest
Everett
Everette
Evergreen
Everitt
Everson
Evert
Everton
Evgen
Evgeni
Evin
Evram
Evren
Evron

Ewald
Ewan
Ewart
Ewell
Ewen
Ewing
Exton
Exzavier
Eyal
Eyan
Ezekiel
Ezell
Ezio

F

Faas
Fabiah
Fabian
Fabien
Fabio
Fabius
Fabricio
Fabrizio
Fadi
Faheem
Fahim
Fahian
Fairchild
Fahin
Faisal
Falco
Falcon
Falk
Fane
Fang
Faolan
Farhan
Farid
Fariji
Faris
Farley
Farol

Faron
Farrell
Farrier
Farrington
Fate
Faulkner
Faunus
Faustino
Fausto
Favien
Fawkes
Fay
Fayette
Fayt
Federico
Fedor
Feivel
Fela
Felice
Feliciano
Feliks
Felipe
Felix
Felton
Femi
Fenix
Fennel
Fennell
Fenris
Fenton
Ferd
Ferdie
Ferdinand
Ferenc
Fergal
Fergus
Ferguson
Fermin
Fernand
Fernando
Fernleigh
Ferran
Ferris
Ferruccio
Feynman
Ffinlo.

Fiacre
Fidel
Field
Fielding
Fife
Figaro
Filemon
Filiberto
Filip
Filipe
Filippo
Filippos
Filius
Fillan
Fillin
Fillmore
Finbar
Finch
Findlay
Fingal
Finian
Finias
Finis
Finlay
Finley
Finlo
Finn
Finnbheara
Finneas
Finnegan
Finnehas
Finnian
Finnick
Finnigan
Finnley
Fintan
Finton
Finvarra
Fionn
Fiore
Fiorello
Firmin
Fisher
Fiske
Fitz
Fitzgerald

Fitzhugh
Fitzpatrick
Fitzwilliam
Fiyero
Flaminio
Flash
Flavio
Flemming
Fletcher
Flint
Florencio
Florentin
Florentino
Florian
Florin
Florizel
Floyd
Flynn
Foivos
Foley
Folsom
Fonzy
Forbes
Ford
Forden
Forest
Forester
Forrest
Forrester
Fortunato
Fosco
Foster
Fotios
Fotis
Fouad
Four
Fox
Foxworth
Foxx
Foy
Foyle
Fran
Frances
Francesco
Francis
Francisco

Franciszek
Franco
Frank
Frankie
Franklin
Franklyn
Franky
Franz
Fraser
Frasier
Frazier
Fred
Freddie
Freddy
Frederic
Frederick
Frederico
Frederik
Fredric
Fredrick
Fredrik
Fredy
Freeman
Freitz
Frey
Friederich
Friedrich
Fritz
Frode
Frodo
Frost
Froylan
Fuad
Fudge
Fulgencio
Fulk
Fulton
Fursey
Fynn

G

Gabe
  Gabin
  Gabino
  Gable
  Gabor
  Gabrian
  Gabriel
  Gabriele
  Gad
  Gadiel
  Gael
  Gaelan
  Gaetano
  Gage
  Gahan
  Gahiji
  Gaige
  Gail
  Gaines
  Gaius
  Galahad
  Gale
  Galen
  Galil
  Galileo
  Gallagher
  Galvin

Galway
Gamaliel
Ganesh
Gannon
Gara
Garcia
Gardener
Gardner
Garen
Gareth
Garett
Garfield
Garin
Garit
Garland
Garlen
Garner
Garnet
Garnett
Garo
Garold
Garrad
Garren
Garret
Garrett
Garrick
Garrison
Garron
Garrus
Garry
Garson
Garth
Garvey
Garvin
Gary
Gaspar
Gaspard
Gaspare
Gaston
Gatien
Gatsby
Gauge
Gaurav
Gauthier
Gaven
Gavin

Gavino
Gavrel
Gavriel
Gavrila
Gavroche
Gavyn
Gawain
Gayle
Gaylon
Gaylord
Geary
Geert
Gehrig
Geiger
Geir
Gelar
Gellért
Gemini
Genaro
Gene
General
Generoso
Genji
Genn
Gennadi
Gennadius
Gennady
Gennarino
Gennaro
Genoah
Gentry
Geoff
Geoffrey
Geoffroy
Geordie
Georg
George
Georges
Georgi
Georgie
Georgio
Georgios
Geovanni
Geraint
Gerald
Geraldo

Gerard
Gerardo
Gerens
Gergely
Gerhard
Gerhardt
Germain
Germaine
German
Gerold
Geronimo
Gerran
Gerrit
Gerry
Gershon
Gershwin
Gert
Gervase
Gerwyn
Gery
Gethin
Gevorg
Ghassan
Gheorghe
Gherman
Ghislain
Giacomino
Giacomo
Giambattista
Giampaolo
Gian
Gianandrea
Giancarlo
Giancarlos
Gianfranco
Gianluca
Gianmarco
Giannes
Gianni
Giannis
Giano
Gianpaolo
Gianpiero
Gianrico
Giasone
Gibb

Gibbes
Gibby
Gibson
Gideon
Gifford
Gijsbert
Gil
Gilad
Gilbert
Gilberto
Gildardo
Gilderoy
Gildo
Gilead
Giles
Gilles
Gillespie
Gilligan
Gillis
Gillon
Gilman
Gilmore
Gilroy
Gino
Gintaras
Gio
Gioacchino
Gioachino
Gioele
Gionata
Giora
Giordano
Giorgino
Giorgio
Giorgos
Giosuè
Giovani
Giovanni
Giovanny
Girolamo
Giuliano
Giulio
Giuseppe
Giustino
Gjergj
Gláucio

Glen
Glendon
Glenn
Glover
Glow
Glyn
Glynn
Godfrey
Godric
Goffredo
Golden
Gomez
Gonçalo
Gonzalo
Goodluck
Goodwin
Gopal
Goran
Gorden
Gordie
Gordon
Gorn
Gösta
Gotama
Gotham
Gottlieb
Gotye
Gough
Govran
Gower
Gracen
Graceson
Gracian
Graciano
Gracin
Graden
Grady
Grae
Graeden
Graeme
Graer
Graf
Grafton
Graham
Grandin
Granger

Granite
Grant
Grantland
Granton
Granville
Gratian
Gratiano
Gray
Grayden
Graydon
Grayley
Graysen
Grayson
Graziano
Green
Greenberry
Greg
Greger
Gregg
Greggory
Gregor
Gregorio
Gregory
Greig
Grey
Greydon
Greysen
Greyson
Griffin
Griffith
Grifin
Grigor
Grigorios
Grigoris
Grimm
Grimmwolf
Grisham
Grissom
Gritt
Grover
Grozdan
Grubbs
Gruff
Gryffin
Gryffyn
Gryphon

Grzegorz
Guadalupe
Gualtiero
Gudmundur
Gudval
Guglielmo
Güicho
Guido
Guilherme
Guillaume
Guillem
Guillermo
Guirec
Guiseppe
Gulliver
Gunnar
Gunner
Gunter
Gunther
Gurdial
Gurgen
Gurinder
Gurkirt
Gurlal
Gurleen
Gurmeet
Gurmej
Gurpreet
Gursagar
Gurtej
Gurwinder
Gus
Gust
Gustaf
Gustas
Gustav
Gustave
Gustavo
Gusten
Guthix
Guthrie
Guto
Guy
Gwilym
Gwylym
Gábor

H

Haakon
Habakkuk
Habib
Hackett
Haddon
Haddow
Haden
Hades
Hadi
Hadleigh
Hadrian
Hadrien
Haegan
Hafiz
Hagen
Hager
Hagop
Haiden
Haidyn
Haig
Haile
Hailen
Hakem
Hakim
Hakob
Hakon
Hal

Halbert
Halcyon
Halden
Hale
Haley
Halil
Hallam
Hallden
Hallie
Hallsten
Halsten
Halston
Haman
Hamed
Hames
Hamid
Hamilton
Hamish
Hamlet
Hammond
Hamp
Hampton
Hampus
Hamza
Han
Handy
Hane
Hank
Hanley
Hanlon
Hanner
Hannes
Hannibal
Hannu
Hans
Hansel
Hanson
Haralampos
Harald
Harambe
Harbhajan
Harbor
Harbour
Hardev
Harding
Hardwin

Hardy
Harish
Harith
Harjeet
Harkin
Harkyn
Harlan
Harland
Harlem
Harlen
Harley
Harlow
Harmon
Harold
Haroon
Harpal
Harper
Harpo
Harrell
Harri
Harriman
Harrington
Harris
Harrison
Harry
Harshaan
Hart
Hartley
Hartwin
Haruki
Harun
Haruto
Harutyun
Harvey
Harvinder
Hasan
Haseeb
Hashim
Hasib
Hasin
Haskell
Hassan
Hastings
Hatcher
Havard
Havelock

Haven
Hawk
Hawken
Hawkeye
Hawkins
Hawthorn
Hawthorne
Hayden
Haydn
Haydrian
Hayes
Haygen
Hayk
Haymitch
Haytham
Hayward
Haywood
Hayworth
Hazen
Hearst
Heartley
Heath
Heathcliff
Heaton
Heber
Hector
Heddwyn
Hedley
Heinrich
Heinz
Heitor
Helaman
Helge
Hélio
Helios
Helix
Helmer
Helmold
Helo
Henderson
Hendrik
Hendrikus
Hendrix
Henley
Hennepin
Hennessy

Henning
Henri
Henrijs
Henrik
Henrique
Henry
Henryk
Henson
Herb
Herbert
Hercules
Heriberto
Herman
Hermann
Hermes
Herminio
Hermon
Hernan
Heron
Herschel
Hersh
Hershel
Hervé
Hervey
Heston
Hewitt
Hezekiah
Hezro
Hezron
Hiawatha
Hibai
Hickory
Hideki
Hideo
Hieronomo
Higinio
Hilaire
Hilario
Hilary
Hilbert
Hillard
Hillary
Hillel
Hilliard
Hilo
Hilton

Hinckley
Hines
Hinto
Hinton
Hipolito
Hira
Hiram
Hiro
Hiroshi
Hirsch
Hirschel
Hirsh
Hisahito
Hisham
Hitoshi
Hixon
Hjalmar
Hjalte
Hlynur
Hoban
Hobart
Hobert
Hodge
Hodges
Hogan
Hogarth
Hoke
Hoku
Holden
Holdyn
Holger
Hollaman
Holland
Hollie
Hollis
Holmes
Holston
Holt
Holton
Homer
Homero
Honor
Honorio
Honorius
Hook
Hooper

Hoover
Hopkins
Hopper
Horace
Horacio
Horatio
Horst
Horton
Hosea
Hoseok
Hosie
Hosteen
House
Houston
Hovhannes
Hovsep
Howard
Howell
Howl
Hoyt
Hrant
Hrayr
Hrishik
Hristo
Hrothgar
Hryhoriy
Huba
Hubert
Huck
Huckleberry
Huddy
Hudson
Huey
Hugh
Hughes
Hughie
Hugie
Hugo
Hugues
Huicho
Huitzilin
Humbert
Humberto
Hume
Humphrey
Hunt

Hunter
Huntington
Huntley
Huntly
Huon
Hurbert
Hurley
Hussein
Huston
Hutch
Hutchison
Hutton
Huw
Huxley
Hyde
Hyman

I

Iago
　Iain
　Iakona
　Iakob
　Iakovos
　Ian
　Ianto
　Iason
　Ib
　Ibo
　Ibn
　Ibraahim
　Ibragim
　Ibraheem
　Ibrahian
　Ibrahim
　Ibrahima
　Ibrahimu
　Icabod
　Icarus
　Ichabod
　Ichiro
　Idan
　Iddo
　Iden
　Ido
　Idris

Ieni
Ieremias
Iestyn
Ieuan
Ifan
Iggy
Ignacio
Ignacy
Ignas
Ignatius
Ignatz
Ignazio
Ignotus
Igor
Ihlas
Ihor
Ihsan
Iisakki
Ikaia
Ikaika
Ike
Ikemefuna
Iker
Ilan
Ilario
Ilarios
Ildefonso
Ilhan
Ilia
Ilian
Ilias
Ilija
Ilir
Iliu
Ilivan
Ilja
Ilya
Ilyas
Imad
Iman
Imanol
Ime
Immanuel
Imran
Imre
Iñaki

Increase
Inderjit
Indiana
Indigo
Indio
Indonesia
Indri
Infinity
Inga-the-swag
Ingo
Ingram
Inigo
Innes
Innocentius
Innocenzo
Innokentiy
Inocencio
Inus
Ioan
Ioannis
Iolaus
Iolo
Ion
Ionas
Ionel
Ionuț
Iordan
Iordanos
Iorwerth
Ioseb
Iosif
Iouis
Ioulianos
Iqbal
Ira
Iraj
Irl
Irrylath
Irvin
Irving
Irwin
Isa
Isaac
Isaak
Isac
Isadore

Isaeah
Isai
Isaia
Isaiah
Isaias
Isaija
Isak
Isambard
Isen
Iser
Ishaan
Isham
Ishmael
Isiah
Isidore
Isidoro
Isidro
Iskender
Isler
Isley
Ismael
Ismail
Isom
Israel
Isreal
Issa
Issac
Issachar
Istvan
Itai
Italino
Italo
Itamar
Ithaca
Ithacian
Itzhak
Iuliu
Ivan
Ivanhoe
Ivanoe
Ivar
Iven
Iver
Ives
Ivey
Ivo

Ivor
Ivory
Ivy
Iwan
Iyler
Izaac
Izaak
Izaiah
Izar
Izaya
Izayah
Izidor
Izik
Izsák
Izzien
Izzy

J

Jaap
    Jabari
    Jabbar
    Jabez
    Jabin
    Jabril
    Jabulani
    Jac
    Jacca
    Jace
    Jacek
    Jacen
    Jachin
    Jacint
    Jacinth
    Jacinto
    Jack
    Jackie
    Jackson
    Jackton
    Jacky
    Jaco
    Jacob
    Jacobi
    Jacobo
    Jacobson
    Jacobus

Jacoby
Jacopo
Jacques
Jad
Jade
Jaden
Jadiel
Jadin
Jadon
Jadran
Jadyn
Jaece
Jaeden
Jaedon
Jaeger
Jafar
Jafet
Jagatpreet
Jagger
Jagit
Jago
Jahan
Jahdani
Jaheem
Jaheim
Jahiem
Jahir
Jahzeel
Jai
Jaiden
Jaidin
Jaidyn
Jaime
Jair
Jairo
Jairus
Jaison
Jakab
Jake
Jakey
Jakin
Jakob
Jakobe
Jakobi
Jakoby
Jaksen

Jakub
Jalal
Jaleel
Jalen
Jalex
Jali
Jalil
Jalon
Jamaal
Jamal
Jamar
Jamarcus
Jamari
Jamarion
Jamarius
Jame
Jameel
Jamel
Jameon
James
Jamesen
Jameson
Jamey
Jamie
Jamil
Jamin
Jamir
Jamisen
Jamison
Jammie
Jamoa
Jamon
Jamys
Jan
Jando
Jandro
Jango
Janika
Janko
Janne
Jannen
Janosch
Janus
Janusz
Janvier
Japhet

Japheth
Jaquan
Jaquez
Jared
Jarek
Jarell
Jarem
Jaren
Jaret
Jareth
Jari
Jarick
Jariel
Jarin
Jarius
Jarlath
Jarle
Jarmo
Jarnail
Jarno
Jarod
Jarom
Jarome
Jaromir
Jaron
Jaroslav
Jarosław
Jarrah
Jarred
Jarrel
Jarrell
Jarres
Jarret
Jarrett
Jarrod
Jarvis
Jasbir
Jascha
Jasdeep
Jase
Jasen
Jasiah
Jasjit
Jaska
Jaskaran
Jason

Jaspan
Jasper
Jaspreet
Jassem
Jasvir
Jaswinder
Jatan
Jaume
Jaune
Javan
Javarion
Javen
Javier
Javion
Javon
Javonte
Jawon
Jax
Jaxen
Jaxin
Jaxon
Jaxsen
Jaxson
Jaxton
Jaxxon
Jay
Jayan
Jaybin
Jayce
Jaycee
Jaycen
Jayceon
Jaycob
Jaydan
Jaydee
Jayden
Jaydin
Jaykob
Jaylan
Jaylen
Jaylin
Jaylon
Jaymar
Jayme
Jaymes
Jayse

Jaysen
Jaysin
Jayson
Jayston
Jayven
Jayvid
Jayvion
Jayvon
Jaziel
Jazz
Jc
Jean
Jeanus
Jeb
Jebediah
Jecey
Jecht
Jed
Jedd
Jedediah
Jedi
Jediah
Jedidiah
Jeevan
Jeff
Jefferey
Jefferson
Jeffersson
Jeffery
Jeffrey
Jeffry
Jehan
Jehu
Jejomar
Jelani
Jelle
Jem
Jemaine
Jemuel
Jencarlos
Jency
Jenkin
Jenner
Jennex
Jennings
Jens

Jensen
Jenson
Jenton
Jeordie
Jeppe
Jepson
Jerad
Jerah
Jerahmy
Jerald
Jeramiah
Jeramie
Jeramy
Jerard
Jere
Jered
Jerel
Jeremey
Jeremiah
Jeremias
Jeremie
Jeremy
Jeret
Jerguš
Jeriah
Jeribai
Jericho
Jerick
Jermain
Jermaine
Jermel
Jerod
Jerold
Jerome
Jeromy
Jeronimo
Jerram
Jerrell
Jerrett
Jerricho
Jerrin
Jerrison
Jerrod
Jerrold
Jerron
Jerry

Jerzy
Jesaiah
Jesiah
Jeson
Jesper
Jess
Jesse
Jessie
Jessine
Jessup
Jessy
Jeston
Jesus
Jet
Jeter
Jethro
Jetson
Jett
Jevic
Jevon
Jewel
Jewell
Jeyden
Jeydon
Jezek
Jhett
Jibril
Jiei
Jim
Jimi
Jimin
Jimmie
Jimmy
Jin
Jinx
Jionni
Jiraiya
Jiri
Jiro
Joab
Joachim
Joah
Joakim
Joan
Joanin
Joaquim

Joaquin
Joar
Joash
Job
Joby
Joc
Jochem
Jock
Jodie
Jodin
Jody
Joe
Joel
Joey
Joffrey
Johan
Johanan
Johann
Johannes
Johdy
John
John Louie
John-Luke
Johnathan
Johnathon
Johnie
Johnnie
Johnny
Johnpaul
Johnson
Jolyon
Jomar
Jomei
Jon
Jonael
Jonah
Jonas
Jonatan
Jonathan
Jonathon
Jondi
Jones
Jonnie
Jonny
Jonty
Joona

Joonas
Jooseppi
Joost
Jorah
Joram
Jöran
Jordain
Jordan
Jorden
Jordi
Jordin
Jordon
Jordy
Jordyn
Joren
Jorge
Jorgen
Jorik
Joris
Jorma
Jorn
Jorvik
Jory
Josafat
José
Jose Luis
Josef
Joselito
Joseluis
Josemaria
Josep
Joseph
Josephus
Joses
Josey
Josh
Joshua
Joshuah
Joshue
Joshy
Josiah
Josif
Josmer
Josmil
Joss
Jostein

Josten
Josué
Jotham
Joules
Jovan
Jovani
Jovanni
Jovanny
Jovany
Jove
Jovi
Jovin
Jovis
Jowan
Joy
Joyce
Jozef
Jozeph
Joziah
József
Jozy
Juan
Juanpablo
Jubal
Judah
Judas
Judd
Jude
Judea
Judge
Judson
Juelz
Juhana
Juho
Juke
Jules
Julian
Juliano
Juliek
Julien
Julij
Julio
Julius
Juliusz
Juma
Jun

Junaid
Junayd
June
Jungkook
Junichiro
Junior
Junious
Junipero
Junius
Junot
Junpei
Jupiter
Juraj
Jurgen
Jurij
Jussi
Justen
Justice
Justin
Justinas
Justino
Juston
Justus
Juuso
Juvenal
Juvencio

K

Kaapro
Kaare
Kabir
Kace
Kacen
Kacey
Kacper
Kade
Kadeem
Kaden
Kadin
Kadir
Kadison
Kadyn
Kaeb
Kaede
Kaeden
Kaedin
Kael
Kaelan
Kaelen
Kaemon
Kaeo
Kafu
Kagan
Kage
Kahlian

Kagen
Kahlil
Kahlilur
Kahlo
Kahnyr
Kahraman
Kai
Kaidan
Kaiden
Kailan
Kailash
Kailer
Kaimana
Kainalu
Kainan
Kaine
Kainen
Kainoa
Kainona
Kairo
Kaiser
Kaison
Kaito
Kaius
Kaiyan
Kaizen
Kaj
Kajus
Kal
Kalan
Kalani
Kale
Kaleb
Kalel
Kalen
Kaleo
Kalib
Kalil
Kalix
Kalle
Kallen
Kallum
Kalman
Kaltag
Kalten
Kalvin

Kamal
Kaman
Kamari
Kamau
Kamden
Kamen
Kameron
Kamil
Kamran
Kamren
Kamron
Kamryn
Kane
Kanen
Kani
Kanoa
Kanwal
Kanye
Kapriel
Karac
Karam
Karamveer
Karan
Karas
Karch
Karcher
Karcsi
Kåre
Kareem
Kari
Karim
Karl
Karle
Karlin
Karlis
Karlos
Karm
Karol
Karolos
Karsen
Karson
Karsten
Karter
Kase
Kasen
Kasey

Kash
Kashton
Kasim
Kason
Kaspar
Kasper
Kassahun
Kassidy
Kassim
Kasyn
Katen
Kato
Kauai
Kavi
Kavin
Kavon
Kawika
Kay
Kayden
Kayen
Kayl
Kaylib
Kaylor
Kayne
Kayode
Kaypha
Kaysa
Kaysen
Kayson
Kayvan
Kayvon
Kazik
Kazim
Kazimierz
Kazimir
Kazuhiro
Kazuki
Kazuo
Kazz
Kdie
Keagan
Keahu
Keali'i
Kealoha
Kean
Keane

Keanu
Kearney
Keary
Keating
Keaton
Keats
Kedrick
Keduse
Keeandre
Keefe
Keegan
Keelan
Keelen
Keeler
Keen
Keenan
Keene
Keenen
Kegan
Keian
Keifer
Keigan
Keiji
Keiman
Keimoni
Keir
Keiran
Keirnan
Keith
Kekoa
Kelan
Kelby
Keldon
Kelemen
Kell
Kellan
Kellen
Keller
Kelley
Kellin
Kelly
Kellynn
Kelsey
Kelson
Kelton
Kelvin

Kelvyn
Kemen
Kemonte
Kemper
Ken
Kenai
Kenan
Kencil
Kendal
Kendall
Kenderick
Kendon
Kendric
Kendrick
Kendry
Kenelm
Kenesaw
Kenji
Kennan
Kennedy
Kennen
Kennesaw
Kenneth
Kennett
Kenney
Kennison
Kennith
Kenny
Kent
Kentekee
Kenton
Kenver
Kenya
Kenyatta
Kenyon
Kenzo
Keola
Keon
Keone
Keoni
Kepha
Kepler
Kerim
Kermit
Kerr
Kerron

Kerry
Kerwin
Keshaun
Keshav
Keshawn
Keshen
Kesiena
Kessler
Kester
Kestyn
Ketan
Kevan
Kevani
Keven
Kevern
Kévim
Kevin
Kevon
Kevork
Kevy
Key
Keyan
Keynan
Keyon
Keyshawn
Kezian
Kfir
Khai
Khaled
Khalid
Khalif
Khalil
Khamari
Khan
Khristopher
Khushwant
Khyree
Ki
Kian
Kiandre
Kiefer
Kiel
Kielan
Kieran
Kieren
Kierian

Kiernan
Kieron
Kierson
Kiev
Kijana
Kikkan
Kilby
Kile
Kilian
Killian
Kilo
Kilohen
Kilroy
Kim
Kimani
Kimball
Kimberly
Kimi
Kimmel
Kimmo
Kincade
Kincaid
Kinchen
Kindin
Kindred
King
Kingman
Kingsley
Kingston
Kinkade
Kinnon
Kinte
Kinter
Kip
Kipling
Kippur
Kipton
Kiptyn
Kiran
Kirani
Kirby
Kiril
Kirill
Kirk
Kirkland
Kirkwood

Kirosh
Kirt
Kit
Kiyan
Kiyle
Kiyoshi
Kjartan
Kjell
Kjetil
Klark
Klaus
Klein
Kline
Klyve
Knight
Knoah
Knowlton
Knowshon
Knox
Knut
Knute
Koa
Koba
Kobe
Kobi
Kobus
Koby
Koda
Koden
Kodiak
Kody
Koen
Kofi
Kogon
Kohana
Kohei
Kohen
Kohl
Koichi
Kojo
Kol
Kolbe
Kolby
Kole
Kolin
Kolohe

Kolten
Kolton
Kolya
Kona
Konner
Konnor
Konrad
Konsta
Konstantin
Konstantine
Konstantinos
Koray
Korben
Korbin
Kord
Koren
Korey
Korin
Kornél
Korosh
Kory
Kosey
Kosmas
Kostandin
Kostas
Kostya
Kostyantyn
Kota
Kouki
Kowen
Kowyn
Koya
Kraig
Kramer
Krasimir
Kreed
Kris
Krisdapor
Krish
Krishna
Krishnan
Krister
Kristian
Kristinn
Kristjan
Kristóf

Kristofer
Kristoff
Kristoffer
Kristofferson
Kristopher
Krisztián
Krisztofer
Kruse
Kruz
Krystian
Kryštof
Krzyś
Krzysztof
Ksawery
Kuba
Kubo
Kubrick
Kubwa
Kuldip
Kullen
Kumail
Kumar
Kunal
Kunta
Kuri
Kurt
Kurtis
Kushaiah
Kwadwo
Kwame
Kwamena
Kwinten
Ky
Kyal
Kyan
Kyden
Kye
Kyeden
Kygo
Kylan
Kyle
Kylen
Kyler
Kyllion
Kylo
Kymani

Kynan
Kyo
Kyon
Kyösti
Kyosuke
Kyree
Kyrie
Kyron
Kyros
Kyrus
Kyrylo
Kyson
Kálmán

L

Laban
Lachlan
Lacrosse
Lacy
Ladd
Lael
Laden
Ladislav
Lael
Laertes
Laeton
Lafayette
Lafe
Laikon
Laird
Laith
Laithian
Lake
Laken
Laketon
Latif
Lakona
Lalit
Lalo
Lamar
Lamarcus
Lambert

Lamberto
Lambros
Lamel
Lamont
Lanark
Lanatir
Lance
Lancelot
Landan
Landen
Lander
Landin
Landis
Lando
Landon
Landrick
Landrum
Landrus
Landry
Landyn
Lane
Laney
Lanford
Langdon
Langston
Langton
Lanigan
Lann
Lannie
Lanny
Lanrick
Larch
Laredo
Laren
Larken
Larkin
Laron
Larry
Lars
Larson
Lashawn
Lasse
Laszlo
Latham
Lathan
Lathel

Lathen
Lathrop
Latif
Latrell
Laughlin
Laurance
Laurel
Lauren
Laurence
Laurencio
Laurent
Laurentinus
Laurenţiu
Laurentius
Lauri
Laurier
Laurin
Laver
Lavern
Laverne
Lavin
Lavonte
Lavoy
Lavrenti
Lavrentios
Law
Lawdon
Lawerence
Lawrance
Lawren
Lawrence
Lawson
Lawton
Laydon
Layne
Layton
Lazar
Lazare
Lazaro
Lazarus
Lazer
Leamon
Leander
Leandre
Leandro
Lear

Leathan
LeBron
Lech
Ledger
Lee
Lee Roy
Leeland
Leen
Leeroy
Leevi
Lefteris
Legend
Legolas
Leib
Leiden
Leif
Leigh
Leighton
Leith
Leizer
Leland
Lelio
Lemon
Lemony
Lemuel
Len
Lenard
Lencho
Lennert
Lennie
Lennon
Lennox
Lenny
Leo
Leocadio
Leon
Leonard
Leonardo
Leonato
Leone
Leonel
Leonhard
Leonid
Leonidas
Leonides
Leopold

Leopoldo
Leotis
Leoton
Lerado
Lerone
Leroy
Les
Lesley
Leslie
Lestat
Lester
Leto
Lev
Levar
Levent
Levente
Leverett
Levi
Leviathan
Levin
Leviticus
Levon
Lew
Lewin
Lewis
Lex
Lexington
Lexon
Leyton
Liam
Liav
Liborio
Librado
Liel
Liev
Light
Lightning
Liir
Liju
Liko
Lilian
Lincoln
Lindel
Lindell
Linden
Lindsay

Lindsey
Link
Linkin
Linley
Linnaeus
Lino
Linsly
Linton
Linus
Linwood
Lion
Lionel
Lior
Lir
Liridon
Liron
Lisandro
Lissandro
Livingston
Liviu
Llewellyn
Llewyn
Lleyton
Lloyd
Llyr
Llywellyn
Lochlan
Lochlyn
Locke
Lockley
Locutus
Loden
Lodewijk
Lodovico
Lofton
Logan
Loïc
Loïck
Loke
Loki
Loman
Lon
Lonán
London
Lonnie
Lonny

Lonzie
Lonzo
Loran
Lorcan
Lorccán
Loren
Lorens
Lorents
Lorenz
Lorenza
Lorenzo
Lorimer
Lorin
Loris
Lorne
Lot
Lothain
Lothair
Loti
Loton
Lou
Louden
Loudon
Louie
Louis
Loukas
Lourenço
Love
Lovell
Lovino
Lowe
Lowell
Lowen
Lowie
Loy
Loyal
Loyd
Luay
Luc
Luca
Lucan
Lucas
Lucca
Lucciano
Lucentio
Lucho

Lucian
Luciano
Lucianus
Lucien
Lucifer
Lucio
Lucious
Lucius
Lucus
Lucy
Ludde
Ludo
Ludovic
Ludovico
Ludvig
Ludwig
Lueis
Lugh
Luigi
Luigino
Luis
Luiz
Luka
Lukas
Luke
Luken
Lukian
Lumen
Luno
Lunsford
Lupe
Lupin
Luther
Lutherum
Lutz
Luuk
Luukas
Luxley
Lyale
Lyall
Lycan
Lydon
Lyle
Lyman
Lyn
Lynden

Lyndon
Lynn
Lynx
Lyon
Lyric
Lysander

M

Mac
    Macalister
    Macario
    Macarius
    Macaulay
    Maccabee
    Maccabi
    Mace
    Macen
    Maceo
    Maciej
    Maciel
    Mack
    Mackee
    Mackendrick
    Mackenzie
    Mackie
    MacKinnon
    Mackland
    Macklen
    Mackson
    Maclain
    Maclean
    Macleod
    Maclin
    Maclovio
    Macon

Macoy
Macsen
Madden
Maddix
Maddock
Maddox
Maddux
Madieu
Madison
Madoc
Madrigal
Mads
Madsen
Maël
Magee
Magglio
Magic
Magne
Magni
Magnum
Magnus
Maguire
Mahdi
Maher
Mahesh
Mahir
Mahlon
Mahmoud
Mahoney
Maicer
Maik
Maine
Mairtín
Maison
Major
Makai
Makaio
Makal
Makana
Makani
Makepeace
Maker
Makhi
Makis
Makishi
Mako

Maks
Maksim
Maksym
Maksymilian
Malachai
Malachi
Malachy
Malak
Malakai
Malaki
Malan
Malaquias
Malcolm
Malcom
Malfoy
Mali
Malik
Malloy
Malo
Malone
Malte
Mamadou
Manasseh
Mandeep
Mandela
Manfred
Maninder
Manish
Manjor
Manjot
Manley
Manly
Mannie
Manning
Mannix
Manny
Manoj
Manolito
Manolo
Manos
Manson
Mansoor
Manu
Manuel
Manus
Manute

Manvel
Manvir
Manzi
Marat
Marc
Marcaeus
Marce
Marcel
Marcelino
Marcell
Marcello
Marcellus
Marcelo
March
Marcial
Marciano
Marcin
Marcio
Marco
Marcos
Marcus
Mardoqueo
Mardy
Marek
Marez
Margarito
Mariano
Marijn
Marileen
Marin
Marino
Mario
Marion
Marios
Marius
Mark
Markel
Markell
Markian
Markku
Marko
Markos
Markus
Marland
Marlei
Marley

Marlin
Marlo
Marlon
Marlow
Marlowe
Marlyn
Maro
Maroney
Marquel
Marques
Marquese
Marquez
Marquis
Marquise
Mars
Marsden
Marshal
Marshall
Marshel
Martell
Marten
Martí
Martim
Martin
Martino
Martinus
Martirio
Márton
Martti
Marty
Martyn
Marvel
Marvin
Marvolo
Marwood
Maryn
Marzio
Masao
Masen
Masis
Mason
Massimiliano
Massimo
Massy
Matas
Máté

Mateen
Matej
Mateja
Mateo
Mateus
Mateusz
Mathéo
Mathew
Mathias
Mathieu
Mathis
Matias
Mats
Matson
Matt
Matteo
Matthan
Matthew
Matthias
Matthieu
Matthijs
Mattia
Mattias
Mattox
Mattson
Matvey
Mátyás
Matys
Mauer
Maurice
Mauricio
Mauro
Maurus
Maury
Maven
Maverek
Maverick
Mavriki
Mawr
Max
Maxden
Maxem
Maxen
Maxence
Maxfield
Maxie

Maxim
Maxime
Maximilian
Maximiliano
Maximilien
Maximillian
Maximino
Maximo
Maximus
Maxon
Maxson
Maxton
Maxus
Maxwell
Maxx
Maxxie
Maynard
Mays
Maysam
Mayson
Mayur
Mazin
Mcarthur
McCauley
McCoy
McKay
McKenzie
Mckinley
McLeod
Mctair
Meade
Mearl
Mederic
Medgar
Mees
Mehcad
Mehedi
Mehdi
Mehmet
Mehrdad
Meir
Mekhai
Mekhi
Mekos
Mel
Melbourne

Melchior
Melchisedec
Melchor
Meletios
Melker
Melky
Mellan
Melton
Melva
Melville
Melvin
Melvyn
Memphis
Menachem
Menahem
Mendel
Menzies
Merald
Merce
Mercer
Mercury
Mercutio
Meredith
Merik
Merit
Meriwether
Merl
Merle
Merlin
Merlyn
Merrick
Merrill
Merritt
Merton
Mervin
Mervyn
Merwin
Meshach
Messiah
Mesut
Methuselah
Mewelde
Meyer
Mic
Micah
Micaiah

Micajah
Michael
Michaiah
Michail
Michal
Michaline
Michalis
Michał
Micheal
Michel
Michelangelo
Michele
Michial
Michiel
Mick
Mickey
Mieczysław
Mienim
Miervaldis
Mies
Miguel
Mihai
Mihail
Mihailo
Mihalis
Mihály
Mihangel
Mihir
Miiltiathis
Mika
Mikael
Mikah
Mikal
Mike
Mikel
Mikey
Mikhail
Mikhol
Mikkel
Mikko
Miklos
Miko
Mikolaj
Mikołaj
Mikyle
Milam

Milan
Milburn
Mile
Miles
Milford
Milias
Millan
Millard
Miller
Milo
Miloh
Milos
Miltiathis
Milton
Mindwell
Miner
Mingus
Minik
Minor
Mio
Miqayel
Miquel
Mircea
Mirek
Miro
Miroslav
Mirren
Misael
Mischa
Mischka
Misha
Miso
Mission
Mitali
Mitch
Mitchel
Mitchell
Mitchum
Mitt
Mitya
Mix
Miłosz
Moctezuma
Modeste
Modesto
Modestus

Modris
Moe
Mohamed
Mohammad
Mohammed
Mohan
Mohandas
Mohil
Mohinder
Mohit
Moise
Moises
Moishe
Moisis
Momiji
Monet
Moni
Monolos
Monroe
Monserrate
Montague
Montana
Montavius
Monte
Montgomery
Monty
Moody
Moon
Moonesar
Mordecai
Mordechai
Mordred
Morgan
Moriarty
Moritz
Morley
Moroccan
Morocco
Moroni
Morpheus
Morrey
Morrie
Morris
Morrison
Morrissey
Morten

Mortimer
Morton
Mose
Moses
Moshe
Moshon
Moss
Mossimo
Mostafa
Movses
Mowgli
Mueez
Muhammad
Mukuro
Mun Chiu
Mungo
Munro
Murad
Murat
Murchadh
Murdoch
Murl
Murphy
Murray
Murry
Musa
Musashi
Mustafa
Myall
Mychal
Mykelti
Myles

N

Naaman
Nabhith
Nabil
Nabin
Nabor
Nacho
Nadav
Nadev
Nadim
Nadir
Naftali
Nahuel
Nahum
Naib
Nain
Nainoa
Nairn
Nairo
Naite
Najee
Nakia
Nakoa
Nakul
Nalin
Nalle
Nam
Naman

Namid
Namin
Namjon
Namjoon
Namon
Nanoq
Naoise
Naos
Naphtali
Napoleon
Narasimha
Narayan
Narciso
Narek
Narpinder
Narrion
Naruto
Nash
Nashua
Nasir
Nat
Nataani
Natale
Natan
Natanaele
Natanel
Nataniel
Natans
Natas
Nate
Nathan
Nathanael
Nathanial
Nathen
Nathyn
Natividad
Naunihal
Navarone
Navarre
Navarro
Naveen
Navraj
Nayan
Nayden
Naydon
Nazaire

Nazar
Nazareth
Nazario
Ndreu
Neah
Neal
Nectarios
Ned
Nedeljko
Needham
Neeko
Neel
Neely
Neftali
Nehemiah
Nehmia
Neil
Neill
Neilson
Neirin
Nellis
Nello
Nels
Nelson
Nemanja
Nemi
Nemo
Neo
Neon
Nephi
Neptune
Neriah
Nerian
Nero
Nery
Nessim
Nestor
Nestore
Netanel
Nevan
Neven
Neville
Nevin
Newell
Newland
Newman

Newton
Neymar
Niall
Nicabar
Nicasio
Nicco
Niccolò
Nicholai
Nicholas
Nicholaus
Nicholson
Nick
Nicklas
Nicklaus
Nickolas
Nicky
Nico
Nicodème
Nicodemus
Nicola
Nicolaas
Nicolae
Nicolai
Nicolaj
Nicolas
Nicolay
Nicolo
Nicomachus
Nielan
Niels
Nien
Nigel
Night
Niilo
Nikaio
Niket
Nikhil
Nikita
Nikko
Niklas
Niklaus
Niko
Nikodem
Nikodemos
Nikola
Nikolai

Nikolaj
Nikolaos
Nikolas
Nikolasz
Nikolaus
Nikos
Niles
Nilo
Nils
Nimkeek
Nimrod
Ninian
Nino
Niraj
Nishan
Nisien
Nissim
Nitai
Nitin
Niven
Nixon
Nizam
Nnamdi
Noah
Noak
Noam
Noble
Noe
Noel
Nogah
Nohl
Nojus
Nolan
Nolen
Nollan
Nomar
Nondas
Nooa
Norayr
Norbert
Norberto
Nori
Norio
Norman
Normand
Norris

North
Northrop
Norton
Norval
Norwood
Nottingham
Nouriel
Nova
Novak
Nuru
Nurul
Nuvan

O

O'Brian
O'Brien
O'Casey
O'Connor
O'Neill
O'Rourke
Oak
Oakland
Oakley
Obadias
Obadiah
Obama
Oban
Obed
Oberon
Oberyn
Obie
Ocean
Oceanus
Ocelotl
Ochuko
Ocie
Octave
Octavian
Octavien
Octavio
Octavius

Oda
Odala
Odd
Ode
Odell
Odern
Odie
Odilio
Odin
Odion
Odis
Odo
Odran
Odubel
Ofydd
Ogden
Ohana
Ohitika
Oisin
Okey
Ola
Olaf
Ólafur
Olajuwan
Olan
Olav
Olavi
Olbracht
Ole
Oleander
Oleg
Oleksandr
Olen
Olev
Olin
Olivander
Oliver
Olivier
Oliviero
Oliwer
Oliwier
Olle
Ollen
Ollie
Ollin
Ollivander

Olliver
Olly
Olmo
Olson
Olu
Omar
Omari
Omarion
Omega
Omer
Omid
Omiros
Omni
Omri
Ondrej
Oneal
Onkar
Onni
Onochie
Ontario
Onyx
Opie
Optimus
Opus
Ora
Oral
Oran
Orange
Orangelo
Orazio
Orel
Oren
Orest
Oreste
Orestes
Orestis
Orev
Orfeo
Orhan
Ori
Orie
Oriel
Orien
Orin
Oriol
Orion

Oris
Orla
Orland
Orlando
Orley
Orlin
Orlo
Orpheus
Orren
Orrie
Orrin
Orry
Orsino
Orson
Ortona
Orval
Orvel
Orvil
Orville
Orvin
Orvon
Orwell
Osama
Osbaldo
Osborne
Osca
Oscar
Oscon
Osian
Osias
Osiris
Oskar
Oskari
Oslo
Osman
Osmar
Osmel
Osmo
Osric
Ossian
Ossie
Osten
Osvaldo
Oswald
Oswaldo
Oswyn

Otey
Otha
Othello
Othmar
Otho
Othon
Otis
Otso
Ottavio
Otten
Ottis
Otto
Oukouaka
Ovadia
Ove
Ovid
Ovidio
Ovidiu
Owain
Owais
Owen
Oxford
Oz
Ozias
Ozuru
Ozzie

P

Paavo
Pablo
Pace
Pacen
Pacey
Packer
Paco
Padarn
Padma
Padraig
Padrig
Paikea
Paisley
Pal
Paladin
Palden
Pall
Palmer
Pancho
Panfilo
Pankaj
Panos
Paol
Paolo
Paora
Parella
Paresh

Parindra
Paris
Park
Parka
Parker
Parkin
Parks
Parkus
Parminder
Parris
Parrish
Parry
Parson
Partab
Parth
Parwinder
Pascal
Pasco
Pascoe
Pascual
Pasha
Pasquale
Pat
Patch
Patrice
Patricio
Patrick
Patrik
Patrizio
Patryk
Patsy
Patten
Patterson
Patton
Pau
Paul
Paulino
Paulo
Pauly
Pavel
Pavlos
Pavol
Pawandeep
Paweł
Pax
Paxtin

Paxton
Payne
Paynter
Payson
Payton
Paz
Peak
Pearce
Pearl
Pearson
Peder
Pedro
Peer
Peerless
Peeta
Peetu
Pek
Peleg
Pelham
Pelle
Pellegrino
Peniel
Penley
Penn
Pennington
Penry
Pepe
Pepito
Per
Percival
Percy
Peregrine
Perez
Pericles
Perico
Perin
Perley
Pernell
Perrin
Perry
Perseus
Pershing
Pervis
Petar
Pete
Peter

peterson
Petr
Petrica
Petroc
Petros
Petrus
Petter
Peyton
Phaedonas
Phaedron
Phaethon
Phaeton
Pharaoh
Pharrell
Pharris
Phelan
Phibes
Phil
Phileas
Philemon
Philip
Philipp
Philippe
Philippos
Phillip
Phillipe
Phillips
Philo
Philomen
Philon
Phinean
Phineas
Phoenix
Phong
Pi
Pierce
Piercy
Pierluigi
Piero
Pierre
Piers
Pierson
Piet
Pietari
Pieter
Pietro

Pike
Pilot
Pinchas
Pinchus
Pink
Pio
Piotr
Pip
Piper
Pippin
Piran
Pirate
Pisa
Pius
Pj
Placid
Placido
Plamen
Platon
Pleasant
Plutarco
Pluto
Poe
Poindexter
Policarpo
Polk
Pollux
Polo
Pompeo
Poncho
Ponciano
Pontus
Porfirio
Porter
Poseidon
Potter
Povel
Powell
Powers
Prabhgun
Prabhjot
Pradeep
Pranav
Pratham
Pratik
Praxedes

Prem
Prentice
Prentiss
Prescott
Presley
Press
Preston
Priam
Price
Priest
Primitivo
Primo
Primus
Prince
Princeton
Pritpal
Proctor
Profit
Proinsias
Prometheus
Promise
Prosper
Prospero
Prudencio
Pryor
Purvis
Pyramid

Q

Qadar
   Qadim
   Qadir
   Qasim
   Qazir
   Quade
   Quaid
   Quannah
   Quentin
   Quenton
   Quest
   Quigley
   Quil
   Quill
   Quillan
   Quillen
   Quin
   Quince
   Quincey
   Quinlan
   Quinn
   Quint
   Quinten
   Quintin
   Quinto
   Quinton
   Quintus

Quique
Quirin
Quirino
Quirt
Quito

R

Raanan
Rabi
Rabin
Rabbi
Rabby
Rabbia
Race
Radames
Radek
Radhak
Radley
Radnor
Radoslaw
Rae
Raeburn
Raed
Raeden
Raekwon
Rael
Raelan
Rafael
Rafal
Rafayel
Rafe
Rafer
Raffaello
Raffee

Rafferty
Raffi
Raghnall
Ragnar
Rahat
Raheem
Rahm
Rahn
Rahsaan
Rahul
Rahyl
Raiden
Raidyn
Raife
Raihan
Raijin
Raimo
Raimondo
Raine
Rainen
Rainer
Rainier
Raiyan
Raj
Rajan
Rajat
Rajjat
Rajeev
Rajendra
Rajesh
Rajib
Rajiv
Rajko
Rajon
Raju
Rakeem
Rakesh
Raleigh
Ralf
Ralph
Ram
Rameen
Rambo
Rameses
Ramesh
Rami

Ramin
Ramiro
Ramiz
Ramon
Ramone
Ramsay
Ramses
Ramsey
Ramy
Ramzi
Rance
Rand
Randal
Randin
Randle
Randolf
Randolph
Randy
Rane
Ranen
Ranger
Raniel
Ranjit
Ranvir
Rannoch
Ransom
Ranulph
Raoul
Raphael
Rasel
Rashad
Rashard
Rashawn
Rasheed
Rashid
Rasil
Rasmus
Raul
Raulo
Raven
Ravenor
Ravi
Rawden
Rawdon
Rawlison
Raxton

Ray
Rayan
Rayburn
Rayce
Rayden
Rayford
Raylan
Raylon
Raymie
Raymon
Raymond
Raymundo
Raynard
Rayner
Raynor
Rayshawn
Rayton
Rayyan
Raz
Raziel
Razmig
Razmik
Re'shawn
Reagan
Reality
Rearden
Reason
Redford
Redmond
Redmund
Reece
Reed
Reef
Reel
Rees
Reese
Reeve
Refugio
Regan
Reggie
Reginal
Reginald
Regis
Regulus
Rehan
Rei

Reid
Reidar
Reife
Reign
Reilan
Reilly
Reimundo
Rein
Reinaldo
Reince
Reiner
Reinhard
Reinhold
Reino
Reis
Rekker
Reko
Rembrandt
Rémi
Remigio
Remo
Remus
Ren
Renaldo
Renard
Renat
Renato
Renatus
Rence
Rene
Renn
Renner
Rennick
Rennon
Reno
Renton
Renzo
Resolved
Reston
Reuben
Reuel
Reunan
Reuven
Revan
Revere
Reverence

Rex
Rexford
Rey
Rey'el
Reydan
Reyden
Reyen
Reyes
Reymundo
Reynaldo
Reynard
Reyner
Reynold
Reza
Rhaegar
Rheal
Rhen
Rhett
Rhidian
Rhoades
Rhodes
Rhodri
Rhone
Rhordan
Rhydian
Rhyland
Rhymer
Rhys
Rhysand
Riaan
Riad
Rian
Riatt
Ricardo
Ricary
Riccardo
Rice
Rich
Richard
Richie
Richmond
Rick
Rickard
Rickey
Ricki
Rickie

Rickon
Ricky
Rico
Rider
Ridge
Ridgley
Ridha
Ridley
Ridwan
Rieden
Rigby
Rigel
Riggan
Riggin
Rigoberto
Rikárdó
Riker
Rikin
Riku
Riley
Rilian
Ringo
Rinnix
Rinzen
Rio
Riordan
Riorden
Riot
Ripkin
Ripley
Rishabh
Rishi
Rishley
Risto
Ritchie
Rito
Ritter
Rivaille
River
Rivers
Riwin
Rixley
Roald
Roan
Roane
Roar

Roark
Roarke
Rob
Robb
Robbe
Robbie
Robby
Robert
Roberto
Roberts
Robertson
Robin
Robinson
Robley
Robrecht
Robson
Roby
Rocco
Roch
Rochen
Rochlan
Rochus
Rock
Rockefeller
Rocker
Rockne
Rocko
Rockwell
Rocky
Rod
Roddy
Rodel
Roderick
Rodger
Rodion
Rodman
Rodney
Rodolfo
Rodolphus
Rodrick
Rodrigo
Roe
Roee
Roel
Roey
Rogan

Rogelio
Roger
Rogerio
Rogers
Rogue
Rohan
Rohen
Rohin
Rohit
Rohn
Roick
Roland
Rolando
Rolf
Rolla
Rolland
Rollie
Rollin
Rollo
Rolph
Roly
Romain
Roman
Romano
Romare
Rome
Romelo
Romeo
Romilly
Romualdo
Rómulo
Romulus
Ron
Ronald
Ronaldo
Ronan
Ronav
Ronen
Ronil
Ronin
Ronnie
Ronny
Rook
Roope
Roosevelt
Roozbeh

Roper
Roque
Roreto
Rorik
Rorimac
Rory
Rosaire
Rosalio
Rosan
Rosario
Roscoe
Rosendo
Rosevelt
Rosh
Roshan
Roshon
Ross
Rossano
Rostam
Rostislav
Roswell
Roth
Rourke
Rouvon
Roux
Rowan
Rowdy
Rowen
Rowland
Rowley
Roxas
Roxby
Roy
Royal
Royce
Royston
Ruairí
Ruairi
Ruaridh
Rubem
Ruben
Rubin
Rudiger
Rudolf
Rudolfo
Rudolph

Rudy
Rudyard
Rueben
Ruel
Ruff
Ruffin
Rufino
Rufus
Ruger
Ruggiero
Rui
Rumen
Rumi
Rumon
Rune
Rupert
Ruperto
Ruprecht
Rush
Rushabh
Rushan
Rushil
Rusik
Ruslan
Russ
Russel
Russell
Rusty
Rutger
Rutherford
Ruxin
Ryan
Ryatt
Ryden
Ryder
Rye
Ryker
Rylan
Rylen
Ryne

S

Saad
  Saava
  Sabas
  Sabastian
  Sabbath
  Sabelo
  Saber
  Sabien
  Sabin
  Sabino
  Sacha
  Sachiel
  Sachin
  Sachio
  Sadaat
  Saddam
  Sadiri
  Sadler
  Sagan
  Sagar
  Sage
  Sahak
  Sai
  Said
  Sailor
  Saimir
  Saint

Sajiv
Sajiva
Sakai
Sakari
Saku
Sal
Saladin
Salahuddin
Salam
Salazar
Saleem
Salem
Salim
Salinger
Salman
Salomon
Salomone
Salvador
Sam
Sama
Samarth
Sameeh
Sami
Samir
Sammie
Sammuel
Sammy
Samoset
Sampo
Sampson
Samson
Samu
Samuel
Samuele
Samuli
Samus
Samvel
Samwise
Sancho
Sandeep
Sander
Sanders
Sanderson
Sandar
Sandro
Sandy

Sanford
Sani
Sanim
Sanjay
Sanjeev
Sanjeewa
Sanjiv
Sansao
Sansone
Santana
Santhosh
Santiago
Santino
Santo
Santonio
Santos
Sarantis
Sarat
Sarell
Sargent
Sargis
Sargon
Sarkis
Sarp
Sascha
Sasha
Sasuke
Satchel
Sathish
Satia
Satin
Saturnino
Satwant
Saul
Saulo
Saurabh
Sava
Saviero
Savio
Savion
Savit
Savvas
Sawyer
Saxby
Saxon
Saxton

Sayer
Sayers
Saylor
Scevola
Schroder
Schroeder
Schuler
Schuyler
Schylar
Scipio
Scooter
Scorpius
Scot
Scott
Scottie
Scotty
Scout
Scully
Seabern
Seager
Seamus
Sean
Seanan
Seanix
Seath
Seathrún
Seattle
Seaver
Seb
Seder
Sedrick
Seeger
Seeley
Seger
Seiji
Selassie
Selby
Selim
Selmer
Selwyn
Sem
Semaj
Semih
Senan
Seneca
Seoras

Seph
Sephiroth
Sepp
Septimus
Seraph
Seraphim
Serge
Sergei
Sergio
Serhat
Serri Rafael
Serry Rafael
Servando
Seryozha
Seth
Seton
Seu
Sevastyan
Seven
Severiano
Severin
Severn
Severo
Severus
Sevin
Seymarion
Seymour
Shad
Shade
Shaden
Shadi
Shadley
Shadow
Shadrach
Shae
Shafer
Shai
Shaikh
Shakespeare
Shalev
Shalom
Shamar
Shamus
Shandy
Shane
Shannon

Shanon
Shantanu
Shaquille
Sharif
Sharnovon
Shasta
Shauftan
Shaughnessy
Shaun
Shauni
Shaw
Shawinook
Shawn
Shay
Shaydon
Shayne
Shea
Shedrick
Shelby
Sheldon
Shelton
Shem
Shemar
Shep
Shepard
Shephard
Shepherd
Shepley
Sheppard
Sheraga
Sheridan
Sherlock
Sherman
Sherrill
Sherwin
Sherwood
Shia
Shiloh
Shimon
Shimshon
Shinon
Shipley
Shirley
Shiva
Shivam
Shlomo

Shmuel
Shohta
Shola
Sholom
Sholto
Shomari
Shon
Showles
Shrek
Shrikant
Shulem
Shye
Shyloh
Shylon
Si
Sian
Siarl
Siarles
Siavash
Sid
Siddarth
Siddharth
Sidney
Siegfried
Sierre
Siger
Sigge
Sigismund
Sigmund
Sigurd
Sigurdur
Silas
Siler
Sillan
Silvan
Silvano
Silvanus
Silven
Silver
Silverio
Silvestre
Silviano
Silvio
Sim
Simão
Simba

Simbiah
Simcha
Simen
Simeon
Simo
Simon
Simone
Simpson
Sinan
Sinbad
Sincere
Sinclair
Sindre
Sindri
Sinhue
Sinjin
Sinqua
Sione
Sipho
Sire
Sirius
Sisamila
Sitka
Sivan
Sivert
Sixten
Skandar
Skate
Skia
Skip
Skipper
Sky
Skye
Skylar
Skyler
Slade
Slaid
Slane
Slate
Slater
Slavko
Slayden
Slayton
Sloan
Slobodan
Sly

Smarth
Smith
Smokey
Snowden
Snyder
Socrates
Soeren
Sofiane
Sofien
Sogoro
Sohan
Sojan
Sojol
Sohrab
Sol
Solace
Solan
Soleil
Soloman
Solomon
Solon
Somerled
Somerset
Sondre
Sonnen
Sonny
Sophian
Sora
Soren
Sorin
Sorley
Sorrell
Sotiris
Soumil
Souta
Spade
Spalding
Sparrow
Spartacus
Spearman
Spellman
Spence
Spencer
Spenser
Spike
Spiro

Spiros
Springer
Spurgeon
Spurrier
Spyridon
Squandro
Squire
St. John
Stacey
Stacy
Stafford
Stahley
Stamm
Stan
Stanford
Stanimir
Stanislas
Stanislaus
Stanislav
Stanislaw
Stanley
Stannis
Stanton
Star
Stark
Starlin
Starsky
Staton
Stavrianos
Stavros
Steele
Stefan
Stefano
Stefanos
Stefen
Steffan
Stein
Steinar
Stejonte
Stelios
Stellan
Sten
Steno
Stephan
Stephanos
Stephen

Stephon
Sterling
Stetson
Stevan
Steve
Steven
Stevenson
Stevie
Stevieray
Stewart
Stian
Stieg
Stig
Stijn
Stiles
Stohn
Stojan
Stokely
Stone
Stoney
Storm
Stormalong
Strand
Stratton
Strauss
Street
Strider
Striker
Stringer
Strom
Struan
Stryker
Stuart
Sturt
Sudhir
Sufjan
Sufyan
Suga
Suhail
Sukhdeep
Sukhvinder
Sukhwinder
Sukrajan
Sulaiman
Sulien
Sullivan

Sully
Sulo
Sultan
Suman
Sumit
Summit
Sumner
Sun
Sundara
Sunil
Sunjit
Sunny
Suraj
Sutter
Sutton
Suvo
Suzaku
Svein
Sveinn
Sven
Sverre
Swain
Swaine
Sweeney
Swinton
Sy
Sydney
Syed
Sykes
Sylar
Sylas
Sylvain
Syrus

T

Tab
   Tabari
   Tabah
   Taber
   Tabor
   Tacitus
   Tacoma
   Tad
   Tadashi
   Taddeo
   Tadeo
   Tadeusz
   Tadhg
   Tadj
   Tadzio
   Taegan
   Taehyung
   Taelyn
   Taemon
   Tafadzwa
   Tafari
   Taft
   Tag
   Taggart
   Taggert
   Taha
   Tahj

Tahmoh
Taiden
Taig
Taiga
Taighan
Taiki
Taine
Taio
Tait
Taiten
Taivan
Taiyo
Taj
Takahiro
Takashi
Takeo
Taki
Takis
Takoda
Takvor
Tal
Tala
Talan
Talbot
Talen
Talford
Talfryn
Taliesin
Tallak
Tallen
Talley
Talon
Talus
Tam
Tamaki
Tamais
Tamer
Tamerlan
Tamerlane
Tamino
Tamir
Tammis
Tanav
Tancredi
Tanek
Taneli

Tangelo
Taniel
Tanish
Tanix
Tankred
Tannen
Tanner
Tannis
Tanrıkut
Tao
Tapinder
Tapio
Tarald
Taran
Taras
Tarek
Tarez
Tarian
Tarick
Tariq
Tariqul
Tarkan
Tarkin
Tarlochen
Tarlock
Tarquin
Tarrant
Tarso
Tarsus
Tarun
Tarus
Tarver
Tarvo
Tarzan
Tasher
Tasker
Tasman
Tassilo
Tatanka
Tate
Tatum
Taul
Taurean
Tauren
Taurus
Tavares

ct22222er

Taven
Tavian
Tavin
Tavion
Tavis
Tavish
Tavon
Tavvi
Tawera
Tayden
Taye
Taylan
Taylen
Tayler
Taylin
Taylon
Taylor
Tayne
Tayo
Tayshaun
Taysom
Tayson
Tayte
Tayton
Taz
Tazz
Teagan
Teaghan
Teague
Teal
Teale
Teancum
Tecumseh
Ted
Teddie
Teddy
Tedric
Teegan
Teemu
Teilo
Telesforo
Télesphore
Telesphoros
Telford
Tellef
Teller

Telly
Temi
Templeton
Tennessee
Tennyson
Tenzin
Teo
Teobaldo
Teodocio
Teodomiro
Teodor
Teodoro
Teodosio
Teodulo
Teofil
Teofilo
Teren
Terence
Terenzio
Terje
Terran
Terrance
Terrell
Terrelle
Terrence
Terrill
Terry
Terzo
Tesher
Teslam
Teunis
Tevel
Tevin
Tex
Texas
Teyo
Th'layli
Thabo
Thackery
Thad
Thaddeus
Thain
Thairgo
Thalen
Thames
Thanasi

Thanasis
Thanatos
Thance
Thane
Thang
Thaniel
Thanos
Thao
Tharold
Thatcher
Thayer
Theadore
Theike
Thelo
Thelonious
Thelonius
Thelxiope
Themistocles
Theo
Theobald
Theobold
Theoden
Theodor
Theodore
Theodoric
Theodosius
Theon
Theophanes
Theophile
Theophilius
Theophilus
Theophrastus
Theosiphus
Theron
Thersander
Theryn
Theseus
Thiago
Thibaut
Thien
Thierri
Thierry
Thijs
Thomas
Thompson
Thomsen

Thor
Thorben
Thordell
Thoreau
Thorfinn
Thorin
Thorn
Thorne
Thornton
Thorstein
Thorsten
Thorvald
Thrace
Thulani
Thurgo
Thurgood
Thurman
Thurston
Ti
Tiaan
Tiago
Tiberias
Tiberiu
Tiberius
Tibet
Tibor
Tiburcio
Tico
Tide
Tidus
Tierce
Tiernan
Tife
Tiger
Tigh
Tighe
Tigran
Tilden
Till
Tillman
Tillo
Tilus
Tim
Timaeus
Timber
Timicin

Timmie
Timmothy
Timmy
Timo
Timoteo
Timotheus
Timothy
Timur
Tin
Tinashe
Tino
Tinsley
Tip
Tippett
Tipton
Titan
Tito
Titus
Tivadar
Tizian
Tiziano
Tizoc
Toben
Tobey
Tobiah
Tobias
Tobin
Tobit
Toby
Tobyn
Tod
Todd
Todor
Toivo
Tokunbo
Tola
Tolek
Tollak
Tolliver
Tolomeo
Tom
Tomache
Tomas
Tomer
Tomias
Tomiche

Tomlin
Tommaso
Tommie
Tommy
Tomokazu
Tomos
Tonatiuh
Toney
Tonino
Tonka
Tono
Tony
Toph
Topher
Topias
Tor
Toran
Torben
Tord
Tore
Toren
Torey
Torez
Toribio
Torin
Torjus
Tormund
Torquil
Torrance
Torrence
Torres
Torrey
Torrii
Torry
Torsten
Torvald
Tory
Toryn
Tosh
Toshi
Toshio
Toulouse
Toumani
Toussaint
Tove
Townes

Townsend
Toy
Trace
Tracey
Track
Tracy
Tradon
Trae
Traece
Traeden
Traian
Traice
Trais
Traisson
Traiton
Trajan
Tranquilino
Traver
Travert
Travis
Travon
Trayce
Trayger
Trayton
Trayvon
Tre
Tredon
Trek
Tremere
Trent
Trenten
Trenton
Treston
Treven
Trever
Trevik
Trevin
Trevion
Trevon
Trevor
Trevyn
Trey
Treyce
Treyden
Treysen
Treyson

Treyton
Treyvon
Trig
Trigger
Trinian
Trinidad
Trinity
Tripp
Trippton
Tristan
Tristen
Tristian
Tristin
Triston
Tristram
Triton
Troah
Tron
Trond
Trotter
Troy
Troyce
Troye
Truan
Truen
Truett
Truitt
Truman
Truth
Trygve
Trym
Trystan
Tuan
Tuck
Tucker
Tudor
Tullis
Tullius
Tulsi
Tumbaghai
Tuncay
Tuomas
Ture
Turi
Turner
Turpin

Tuscan
Tuur
Twain
Ty
Ty-Nassir
Tybalt
Tyce
Tychicus
Tycho
Tychon
Tye
Tygan
Tyger
Tyko
Tylen
Tyler
Tyler.
Tylon
Tylor
Tyme
Tymon
Tymoteusz
Tynan
Tyner
Tyquan
Tyr
Tyree
Tyreek
Tyreese
Tyrel
Tyrell
Tyrese
Tyrian
Tyric
Tyrion
Tyriq
Tyrion
Tyrus
Tyson
Tzvi

U

Udo
  Udoka
  Ugo
  Uhuru
  Uilleam
  Uisne
  Ulf
  Ulises
  Ulrich
  Ulrik
  Ultan
  Ulysses
  Umar
  Umberto
  Umut
  Unai
  Upton
  Urban
  Urbano
  Urelio
  Urho
  Uri
  Uriah
  Urias
  Uriel
  Uriele
  Urijah

Uriyah
Usain
Usher
Usko
Usman
Utah
Uther
Uvaldo
Uzi
Uzzi
Uziah
Uzziah

V

Vadden
Vadim
Vagn
Vahan
Vaisa
Val
Vale
Valen
Valens
Valente
Valentim
Valentin
Valentine
Valentino
Valerian
Valerio
Valerius
Valiar
Valin
Valon
Valor
Valter
Valtteri
Van
Vance
Vanden
Vander

Vanek
Vanhi
Vansen
Vanya
Vardan
Vardinon
Vardis
Varian
Varick
Varren
Varro
Varun
Vasanta
Vasche
Vasco
Vasek
Vash
Vasil
Vasile
Vasili
Vasilios
Vasilis
Vasily
Vaslav
Vassilis
Vassily
Vasyl
Vaughan
Vaughn
Veeti
Vegard
Vegas
Veit
Venn
Ventura
Venustiano
Verdell
Verdi
Vere
Vergil
Verl
Verle
Verlin
Vern
Vernal
Vernay

Verne
Vernell
Verner
Vernie
Vernon
Vernor
Versilius
Vertumnus
Veselin
Veselko
Vester
Vetle
Vexen
Vian
Vicente
Vickery
Victor
Victoriano
Victorino
Vidal
Vidar
Vidyut
Viggo
Vihaan
Vijay
Vikas
Viking
Vikram
Viktor
Vilen
Vilhelm
Vilho
Viljami
Viljo
Vilko
Vill
Ville
Villian
Vin
Vinay
Vince
Vincenc
Vincent
Vincenzo
Vinchenzo
Vine

Vinh
Vinicio
Vinnie
Vinny
Vinson
Vinton
Vinze
Virgil
Virgilio
Virgle
Vishal
Vitaly
Vito
Vitor
Vitorino
Vittore
Vittorio
Vitus
Vivek
Vivian
Viviano
Viyan
Vladilen
Vladimir
Vladislav
Vlaho
Vlasios
Vlastimir
Vogel
Vojtech
Voldemort
Volker
Volney
Von
Voss
Vrai
Václav

W

WADE
Wagner
Wahed
Wahid
Waino
Waite
Wake
Waker
Waldemar
Walden
Waldo
Waleed
Walenty
Walid
Walker
Wallace
Wally
Walsh
Walt
Walter
Walther
Walton
Ward
Wardell
Warden
Ware
Warner

Warren
Warrick
Wasif
Wasim
Wassily
Wasyl
Watkins
Watson
Watt
Waverly
Wavie
Wayde
Wayland
Waylon
Waymon
Wayne
Waziri
Weaver
Webb
Webster
Weiquan
Weldon
Wellington
Wells
Welton
Wendell
Wentworth
Wenzel
Werner
Wernher
Wes
Weslan
Weslee
Wesley
Wesson
West
Westin
Westley
Weston
Weylin
Whakaio
Wheeler
Wheelock
Whelan
Whidbey
Whistler

Whitaker
Whitfield
Whitman
Whitney
Whittaker
Whyatt
Widopson
Wieland
Wiktor
Wilber
Wilberforce
Wilbert
Wilbur
Wilburn
Wild
Wilde
Wilder
Wiley
Wilford
Wilfred
Wilfredo
Wilfrid
Wilhelm
Wilkes
Will
Willam
Willard
Willem
William
Williams
Willie
Willis
Willison
Willoughby
Wills
Willum
Willy
Wilmer
Wilmot
Wilson
Wilton
Wim
Win
Wincenty
Windell
Windradyne

Windsor
Winfield
Winford
Winfred
Winslow
Winsor
Winston
Winter
Winthrop
Winton
Wisdom
Witold
Witt
Wladimir
Wmffre
Wohali
Wojciech
Wole
Wolf
Wolfe
Wolfgang
Wolfie
Wolfram
Wolodymyr
Wondimu
Wood
Woodrow
Woodson
Woody
Woolsey
Worth
Wout
Wren
Wrenn
Wright
Wyatt
Wyeth
Wyitt
Wyland
Wylie
Wyman
Wyn
Wynden
Wyndham
Wynton

X

Xan
    Xano
    Xadrian
    Xander
    Xane
    Xanthus
    Xaver
    Xavi
    Xavier
    Xavior
    Xayden
    Xenon
    Xenophon
    Xenos
    Xoan
    Xyan
    Xyler
    Xzavier

Y

Yada
Yadon
Yael
Yahir
Yahya
Yair
Yaisir
Yaison
Yakir
Yakov
Yakup
Yale
Yancy
Yandel
Yandiel
Yanis
Yann
Yanni
Yannick
Yannig
Yannis
Yaphet
Yaqub
Yarden
Yared
Yariel
Yarrow

Yash
Yasser
Yatika
Yavor
Yazan
Ybarra
Yeats
Yechiel
Yefet
Yehuda
Yehudah
Yered
Yericho
Yervant
Yeshua
Yestin
Yidel
Yinshií
Yisrael
Yisroel
Yitzhak
Ylenio
Ymir
Yngwie
Ynyr
Yoav
Yoel
Yohan
Yona
Yonah
Yonatan
Yoni
Yorick
York
Yoruba
Yosef
Yoshio
Yossel
Yosuke
Youking
Young
Yousef
Yovan
Yovanni
Ysidro
Yudel

Yuji
Yul
Yule
Yuli
Yulian
Yunus
Yurek
Yurem
Yuri
Yuriel
Yuriy
Yusef
Yusuf
Yves
Ywain

Z

Zabe
  Zabbar
  Zabin
  Zac
  Zacary
  Zach
  Zachariah
  Zacharias
  Zacharie
  Zachary
  Zachery
  Zack
  Zackary
  Zackery
  Zade
  Zaden
  Zadock
  Zadok
  Zaeem
  Zaen
  Zafar
  Zahavi
  Zaid
  Zaidan
  Zaiden
  Zaim
  Zain

Zaire
Zak
Zakaree
Zakary
Zakeriah
Zaki
Zakiah
Zakk
Zale
Zalman
Zameer
Zampher
Zander
Zane
Zani
Zaniel
Zannon
Zaphod
Zaran
Zarek
Zahin
Zarir
Zarko
Zarley
Zavian
Zavien
Zavier
Zavin
Zavion
Zavior
Zaxon
Zayd
Zayed
Zayden
Zayenthar
Zayin
Zaylen
Zayn
Zayne
Zayrian
Zbigniew
Zdravko
Zeal
Zeb
Zebastian
Zebedee

Zebediah
Zebulon
Zebulun
Zechariah
Zed
Zedekiah
Zedrick
Zef
Zeferino
Zeff
Zeke
Zeki
Zekki
Zelek
Zelig
Zeljko
Zen
Zenith
Zennor
Zeno
Zenon
Zephan
Zephaniah
Zephyn
Zephyr
Zeppelin
Zepplin
Zerach
Zerah
Zeref
Zerek
Zeth
Zethar
Zeus
Zev
Zevan
Zeven
Zevin
Zevon
Zevran
Zezima
Zhenya
Ziad
Zion
Ziri
Ziv

Ziyad
Zizi
Zodiac
Zoilo
Zollie
Zoltan
Zoran
Zoravar
Zoriah
Zorion
Zosimus
Zotique
Zowie
Zubin
Zuko
Zuzen

CONCLUSION & RESOURCES

THANK you once again for purchasing this baby names book, and we hope you were able to find some favorites.

If you are interested in searching a particular name to see how its popularity has changed over time, and see the name's meaning, go to the Baby Name Wizard website at bitly.com/namewizard

Also, if you enjoyed this book and are able to leave us a review on Amazon, we'd appreciate your honest feedback. You can leave a review by searching for this book on Amazon or visiting your previous Orders page.

If you found an error in this book or have a suggestion for improvement, please email editor Katie Clark at contact@walnutpub.com.

Good luck in your parenting journey!